Lenamay Green

A Girl's Journey through Europe, Egypt and the Holy Land

Lenamay Green

A Girl's Journey through Europe, Egypt and the Holy Land

ISBN/EAN: 9783744762472

Printed in Europe, USA, Canada, Australia, Japan

Cover: Foto ©Andreas Hilbeck / pixelio.de

More available books at **www.hansebooks.com**

A GIRL'S JOURNEY

THROUGH

EUROPE, EGYPT

AND

THE HOLY LAND.

PRINTED FOR THE AUTHOR.
PUBLISHING HOUSE OF THE M. E CHURCH, SOUTH.
J. D. BARBEE, AGENT, NASHVILLE, TENN.
1889.

TO
MY DEAR FATHER AND MOTHER,
WHO SO KINDLY GAVE ME THE TRIP,
THIS VOLUME IS
AFFECTIONATELY DEDICATED.

INTRODUCTION.

My niece, Lenamay Green, has written a book of travels that will be read. A book just like it has never been published before. A girl of eighteen kept a journal of her tour through Europe, Egypt, and the Holy Land, without a *dream* of authorship. Some of her home letters took air through the newspapers, and now everybody wants the journal printed. Relatives, friends, publishers, and the daily press have all urged the printing of this volume. Here it is, beautifully illustrated and handsomely bound. Miss Green was with me abroad for nearly twelve months. After her graduation at the Columbia Athenæum she had read up for the trip, and entered upon it with a glow of enthusiasm. She was an unflagging traveler and sight-seer, and never failed to record her impressions. They were the impressions of an intelligent and thoughtful girl, as you will plainly perceive by reading this book. Miss Green accompanied my family everywhere, and while I was looking at objects with a pair of old eyes she kept a pair of young eyes very wide open. Read this handsome volume, and see if she did not! Miss Green is the daughter of Rev. William M. Green, D.D.

R. A. YOUNG.

CONTENTS.

	PAGE
INTRODUCTION	5

CHAPTER I.
Nashville to New York—The Voyage......... 11

CHAPTER II.
From Queenstown to Killarney............... 19

CHAPTER III.
Limerick—Dublin—Portrush—Glasgow......... 27

CHAPTER IV.
Trosachs—Stirling—Edinburgh................ 35

CHAPTER V.
London 45

CHAPTER VI.
From London to Brighton.................... 56

CHAPTER VII.
Paris....................................... 67

CHAPTER VIII.
Marseilles—Mediterranean Sea............... 82

CHAPTER IX.
Alexandria.................................. 90

CHAPTER X.
Cairo—Pyramids............................. 97

CHAPTER XI.
Heliopolis—Cairo........................... 109

Chapter XII.
Steamer "Rahamanier"—Jaffa—Jerusalem........ 116

Chapter XIII.
Jericho—Dead Sea—River Jordan............... 130

Chapter XIV.
Jerusalem—Bethlehem—Jaffa.................... 139

Chapter XV.
Steamer "Ceres"—Beyroot—Smyrna............. 151

Chapter XVI.
Constantinople—Athens........................ 160

Chapter XVII.
Corfu—Brindisi—Naples—Pompeii.............. 174

Chapter XVIII.
Rome—Christmas............................... 188

Chapter XIX.
Florence...................................... 206

Chapter XX.
Pisa—Genoa—Milan............................ 215

Chapter XXI.
Venice.. 225

Chapter XXII.
Vienna—Prague................................ 239

Chapter XXIII.
Dresden—Leipzig—Wittenberg.................. 249

Chapter XXIV.
Berlin.. 256

Chapter XXV.
Potsdam—Hamburg.............................. 266

Chapter XXVI.
Copenhagen—Hanover........................... 276

Chapter XXVII.
Rotterdam—The Hague—Delfthaven 286

Chapter XXVIII.
Amsterdam—Haarlem—Leyden 295

Chapter XXIX.
Antwerp—Brussels—Cologne 302

Chapter XXX.
River Rhine—Coblentz—Mayence 311

Chapter XXXI.
Wiesbaden—Frankfort—Worms 318

Chapter XXXII.
Heidelberg—Baden-Baden—Strasburg 324

Chapter XXXIII.
Basle—Lucerne—Berne 330

Chapter XXXIV.
Interlachen—Lausanne—Geneva 338

Chapter XXXV.
Paris Again 348

Chapter XXXVI.
London 358

Chapter XXXVII.
Windsor—Eton—Stoke-Pogis—Oxford 367

Chapter XXXVIII.
Leamington—Kenilworth—Stratford 375

Chapter XXXIX.
Chester—Liverpool 383

Chapter XL.
The Voyage Home 390

ILLUSTRATIONS.

	PAGE
Frontispiece.	
Edinburgh Castle	38
Tomb of Napoleon	74
Scene on the Nile	102
The Sphinx	105
One of Our Donkeys	112
Jerusalem	122
Lepers Outside Jerusalem	124
Approaching the Mosque of Omar	126
Ford of the Jordan	136
Bethlehem	138
Jews' Wailing-place	145
A House-top in the East	147
Constantinople	162
The Acropolis	168
Pompeii	178
The Coliseum	194
Leaning Tower at Pisa	216
Venice	226
Bridge of Sighs	228
Scene in Venice	232
Dutch Wind-mill	287
Bear-pit	336
Swiss View	342
St. Paul's Cathedral	364
Windsor Castle	368
Warwick Castle	376
Shakespeare's Birthplace	378

A GIRL'S JOURNEY.

CHAPTER I.

NASHVILLE TO NEW YORK—THE VOYAGE.

WERE you ever playfully told, "Go to Jericho?" and did you ever think seriously of the long journey over land and sea to that strange old city that *was* and *is* not? Now I propose to tell how I, a girl of eighteen, fresh from school, eager for the novelty and excitement of travel, sailed away, away, into the far-off Orient, terminating my journey at the Dead Sea and the site of ancient Jericho.

I was so fortunate as to join a party which consisted of Dr. R. A. Young and wife and their daughters, Mary Green and Susie Hunter; to be augmented later by Mr. and Mrs. Charles Eastman, of Nashville, Tenn. I shall not weary you with a description of our parting with the host of friends gathered one sultry afternoon in August at the Union Depot in Nashville to bid us good-by. If such a thing had been possible, enough good wishes followed us to float our ship, the "**Umbria**." The last farewell being spoken, our train steamed out into the night, and we were fairly on our way, leaving home and friends behind. Next morning we passed through Cincinnati, and the following day reached Washington City in time for breakfast. Of course we took in the sights of the capital, though most of the party had visited it before.

Evening found us—tired, hungry, and dusty—wending our way to the Grand Central Hotel, in New York City. We were thankful to rest, even with the never-ceasing roar of Broadway sounding in our ears.

The next two days were spent in sight-seeing and shopping in the great metropolis.

We girls staid up nearly all the night before sailing, puzzling over the problem of how to make a large valise hold as much as a small trunk. Perseverance conquered, and we went to sleep at last with the satisfaction of knowing that all the necessary articles had been packed, and every thing made ready for the voyage. Our trunks had to go into the hold of the vessel, so would be of no use to us until we landed.

Several friends were at the wharf to see us off, and went with us on an exploring expedition through the steamer, from engine-room to promenade deck. It was a wonderful sight, and we were highly entertained.

On Saturday afternoon, just before the vessel started, the scene was most exciting. Hundreds of people were there, shouting and waving farewells—some laughing, others crying, and a few seemingly indifferent.

At three o'clock we moved off, and getting out our glasses enjoyed the splendid view of the city and harbor as they slowly faded from sight.

How we had dreaded the voyage! We girls had made up our minds to be seasick in spite of the perfect weather with which we were favored. The ocean was calm as a lake, and everybody staid on deck from morning until time for retiring at night.

After breakfast on Sunday Captain McMickin read prayers in the dining-saloon, and the rest of the day was spent by the passengers in lounging about, dozing, talking, reading, and occasionally promenading up and down the decks.

After dinner we three girls were taking a "constitutional" on the promenade deck, when the sound of music was heard in the distance. On searching around we discovered that it came from below, and immediately descended to the lower deck, where we saw a number of steerage passengers gathered together singing hymns. In the midst of them, with a baby on her lap, was Ellen Terry, the great English actress, who was returning from a pleasure-trip to America. She was leading the songs with her clear, sweet soprano, and as the familiar tunes rolled out over the water we found ourselves joining in, and were benefited and cheered by the simple home-music. The sailors sung too, many of them perched upon the railing, and often applauded when a favorite song was rendered; some of them had fine voices and seemed to enjoy the music immensely, singing lustily, and evidently with their whole souls.

After becoming accustomed to the routine on shipboard we found that a sea-voyage *could* be pleasant after all. Our steamer, the "Umbria," was elegantly furnished, and had all the conveniences desired. There were five stories, or decks, to the vessel—first and lowest, the hold; then the main deck; above that the saloon deck, where the dining-saloon and our state-rooms were; next, the upper deck; and highest of all, the promenade deck, where we spent the time during the day in our steamer chairs.

One of the young lady passengers called us girls "the nuns," because we were always so covered and bundled up in hoods, veils, cloaks, jackets, etc. Though it was August, the sea-breezes were quite cool, and we did not feel uncomfortable under all our wraps.

One morning everybody on deck was looking rather sleepy and stupid, and every thing was quiet and still when somebody cried: "A whale!

a whale!" You should have seen how those shawls, rugs, veils, glasses, books, and cloaks were dashed aside as we rushed excitedly to the railing to see the wonder. Two whales kindly came up and spouted for our amusement, and I think there was more than one passenger who, besides being glad of a sight of these monsters of the deep, secretly exulted that here at last was an item for the journals, which, on account of the tedium of ocean life, were becoming rather monotonous. We also saw several porpoises and some sea-gulls.

One evening we had a concert in the dining-hall, given by the passengers and sailors for the benefit of the "Liverpool Seamen's Orphanage." Henry Irving, the actor, who was also one of our fellow-passengers, served as chairman, and Miss Terry, dressed in quite a picturesque tea-gown, took up a collection in the captain's hat. The principal features of the entertainment were some mandolin solos, a song by one of the sailors, and the funniest music that I ever heard on a bagpipe; it was so jolly and ridiculous that the whole audience applauded and laughed until their sides ached. Then, too, Mr. Irving gave us a very amusing little speech and recitation combined.

Our walks on the promenade deck were quite a rest, and we managed to get a good deal of fun out of them, owing to the fact that sometimes the wind was so strong it was difficult to keep on our feet, and several amusing encounters resulted. We "nuns" were dashing frantically along one day, trying to "make time," when, turning a corner rather suddenly, I was precipitated into the arms of an astonished youth, who was so much amazed at my extraordinary caper that he did not even inquire what was the matter. Of course I was very much embarrassed, and, after begging his pardon, retreated as hastily as I came. Another time I nearly ran over the captain, which would indeed have been a sad catastrophe.

One day Susie and I went down to see the sailors, who while off duty were at their games. Two of them had their hands and feet tied to a stick, which was passed under their knees, and each tried to push or kick the other out of the ring. Sometimes they rolled over and over, and when they got on their backs, as they did occasionally, it was difficult for them to get righted. They laughed and shouted like a lot of school-boys, and did not seem to be the least out of humor with each other. A favorite game with the passengers was quoits.

Though we had been so fortunate on our voyage, having almost entirely escaped the dreaded seasickness, and though we had been favored with fine weather, we were not grieved when at the end of six days and thirteen hours the time came to pack up and make ready for leaving the steamer. The glasses were brought out, and we strained our eyes to catch a first glimpse of the shores of Erin.

CHAPTER II.

FROM QUEENSTOWN TO KILLARNEY.

AT about seven o'clock Saturday morning land was sighted, and at eleven we left the "Umbria" for a little steam-tug, which conveyed us and our baggage to the shore in about an hour and a half. How grand the old ship looked as she steamed off into the ocean again, all the passengers and crew waving and shouting to us from the decks! We felt quite small and insignificant in our tiny tug by the side of that iron monster. From the vessel the shores of Ireland seemed cut up into small squares and patches no larger than one of our gardens at home. These little plots, we discovered on approaching nearer, were farms, beautifully cultivated, and divided from each other by hedges or stone walls, very few fences of any kind being used. We should have known without being told that this was the *Emerald Isle*, for it was *green, green,* everywhere; so restful and refreshing to the eyes after the monotony of the ocean.

The first person we met on shore was an old Irishwoman who handed each of us a sprig of shamrock, and in return demanded a penny, which was very willingly given.

We had some fun at the custom-house. The officer was quite a pleasant-looking young fellow, and, when we gravely informed him that our valises contained neither spirits nor tobacco, told us that it was not necessary to open our sachels — merely glanced into the trunks, and ornamented every thing with the useful little chalk-mark; but we saw him going through one man's trunk, examining bundles and boxes very carefully.

We went by rail from Queenstown to Cork, passing on the way the castle of "Groat," which means *four pence.* This castle was built by an old lady who paid her workmen in supplies; and she managed so well that the building really cost only four pence in money.

At the station in Queenstown we were constantly amused by the shrill little whistles on the locomotives. They sounded like toy whistles, and we girls could but laugh when we heard them. The cars also were much smaller than we were accustomed to at home.

In our carriage, or coupe, as they call the railway cars, were an Irish gentleman and his two daughters who lived at Queenstown. We saw their residence as we passed along, and it was quite a pretty place. They were very pleasant people, and told us some interesting things about the country.

After changing cars at Mallow and passing through miles of beautiful green country we reached Killarney late in the afternoon, and drove out to the Victoria Royal Hotel, which is situated so as to command a lovely view of the lower lake. The turf was studded with beds of gorgeous flowers, and sloped gently down to the water's edge.

One end of the dining-room was of glass, revealing a fairy-like scene consisting of the little islands of the lake, and the purple haze of the mountains in the background.

How still every thing was! and how queer and old-fashioned the furnishings of the house! We examined our rooms with a great deal of interest. The beds were very high and very "fat," with ruffles around the bottom. We had to climb into them from a chair. There were old-fashioned dressing-cases, also ruffled; and the queerest of window-shades, chests of drawers, bell-ropes, and curtains.

We dressed for the seven o'clock dinner by candle-light—our first experience with this mode of illumination, and Susie claimed the exclusive privilege of using the snuffers.

I must describe our initiatory *table-d'hote* meal in Europe. At each place were three or four glasses, a number of knives, forks, and spoons, several plates—two or three, I believe —and a dark-looking roll, or bun, wrapped up in a napkin. Soup was served first, then the fish, and next a little greasy cake with a small fish in the middle of it; after that some kind of fowl, exactly what I could not decide. This was followed by a course of ham, potatoes, veal, and some green things that looked like *grasshoppers*, but which proved to be French beans. For dessert we had something on the order of ginger-pudding, only it was bitter, and some rice covered with sauce that looked and tasted more like red ink than any thing I could think of. I only tried one morsel, and found I did not want that. Next, cheese and crackers; but as I did not recognize what they were, or know how to get them out of the dish, that course was allowed to pass. We finished on fruit—tiny apples and plums. I cannot say that I enjoyed all nine courses, but managed to exist until breakfast.

The table extended the whole length of the room, with pots of ferns and coleus-plants down the center. The silver was old-fashioned and dumpy, and the table linen spotless, glossy, and real Irish. Everybody was served at once in a dignified and stately manner, and altogether I do not know that I ever felt quite so solemn and subdued. I would not have laughed aloud for any amount, and thus run the risk of being glared at by those august Irish and English dames.

After dinner we found a *London Times* in the drawing-room, and read with interest an account of the dreadful Charleston earthquake, which had occurred while we were on the ocean.

Next morning, after a ten-o'clock breakfast, we put on heavy wraps, as the wind was quite cool, and wandered down to the lake, the beauty of which I cannot describe. On our return a ride was suggested, and we ladies got into an Irish jaunting-car—a jolly little vehicle, holding four persons and a driver, with the backs of the seats together. We drove out to Ross Island, where are the ruins of Ross Castle, an old gray stone building, partly tumbled down, and overgrown with ivy.

The whole of the county (Kerry) is owned by the Earl of Kenmare, whose new country mansion we saw during our drive.

Mary G. said the prettiest things she saw were the tiny donkeys; they were "so cute and sleepy looking." Very often one of them would be drawing a cart on which was piled a whole Irish family and all their marketing.

Another curiosity was the monkey puzzle-trees. They had one long trunk like a monkey's tail, with a *lot* of little tails branching out from the sides and curling up at the ends. We asked our guide, or driver, if they had any corn in that country. At first he did not seem to understand, but when we said "*Indian* corn," he replied: "Yes, I have seen some in the Earl of Kenmare's green-house." He had never heard of sweet potatoes.

We girls became so much amused at the stillness and solemnity of every thing in the drawing-room after dinner that we all, with one accord, rushed precipitately from the room and dashed upstairs to have our laugh out, and thus prevent an undignified explosion before all the grand company.

It was so nice to go to sleep at night on a soft bed that did not toss us from side to side; to have plenty of room to walk around; not to be disturbed by the roar of the steamer's machinery, and to awake in the morning and look out of a window that was *something* larger than a dinner-plate.

As it was raining on Monday, we concluded not to prolong our stay at Killarney, as there would be no chance for excursions on the lake. They say there that their rainy spells generally last about ten days, and that they have "three or four of them a month." No wonder Ireland is so green!

CHAPTER III.

LIMERICK—DUBLIN—PORTRUSH—GLASGOW.

RAIN fell nearly all the time we were in Limerick, so our impressions of the place were decidedly *damp*. The principal point of interest was the old cathedral of St. Mary. As the chimes are rung only on Sunday, we did not hear them; but we went through the church, seeing many ancient tombs and monuments. It was very cold that first night in Limerick; and after sitting on the floor, writing up our journals by the dim light of one *solitary* candle, we hurried to bed in order to get warm.

It was raining as usual next morning; but we set out, equipped with cloaks and umbrellas, to see something of the city. After wandering around, peeping into several churches, and trying to protect ourselves from the beggars (horrible-looking creatures who blessed us if we gave them a penny, and cursed us with equal vehemence if we did not), we found our way into quite a pretty little park, from which place the rain drove us back to the hotel.

Just before leaving for the station we bought some Irish point-lace handkerchiefs from a poor, wretched-looking old woman, who said she had been working in lace for thirty-six years. They were very pretty, with a row of shamrock leaves worked round the border, and an Irish harp in each corner.

Leaving Limerick in the rain, we passed on to Dublin. By the way our train stopped at a little station called Kildare, of which "sweet Jenny," in the song, was "the flower." I felt tempted to stop awhile in this quiet, shady little nook, but there was no time for tarrying.

In Dublin we were delightfully quartered at the Gresham Hotel. After dinner we walked up Sackville Street, past the O'Brien, Bright, Nelson, O'Connell, and King William monuments, also Trinity College and the old Parliament building, now used as the Bank of Ireland.

On the way back we bought some Irish candy, which I did not think equal to American confectionery.

In our rooms that night we felt quite rich, with *two* candles for illumination and a set of steps from which to climb into bed.

On Wednesday we "did the town," as our English friends would say. First we went to St. Patrick's Cathedral, where, besides many old tombs and statues, is the slab which marks the last resting-place of Dean Swift and his Stella. Each of us sat in a chair made from the roof of the old church said to have been built by St. Patrick himself. They gave us a drink of cool water from St. Patrick's well, which is inside the building. After a delightful drive through Phœnix Park we visited the Zoological Gardens, and then went to see the tomb of that great Irish patriot, Daniel O'Connell; also drove past the house where Thomas Moore was born. Phœnix Park is quite large, but it seemed to me rather bare and sunny. I think that more English oaks would improve it.

After an early breakfast our line of march was resumed—this time toward Portrush by the way of Londonderry and Coleraine. The country looked much the same as the south of Ireland, except that a little more care and thrift were displayed in its cultivation.

The hotel at Portrush was new, and kept something on the American plan. We had chicken for dinner—the first since leaving home.

Bright and early next morning we took a car and drove out eight miles to the Giant's Causeway. The road, for some distance, lay along the sea-shore, and the views from different points were beautiful. Getting out of the car on the way, we walked down to the great rock where is the "Wishing Arch." Another curiosity was the "Devil's Punch-bowl," but as I rolled head-foremost down a small hill on the way to it, my recollections of his Satanic majesty's drinking-vessel are rather vague and confused.

Leaving the car at the Causeway Hotel, we secured a guide, and clambered down over the rocks into a small boat, so as to take our first view from the water. Some of the party, however, did not like the rolling and plunging of our little craft, so we rowed ashore and walked round another way. I was rather disappointed at the first view, but the nearer we approached the more wonderful it became, and I felt fully repaid for all the rough climbing and "tumbling" that I had undergone.

We were shown, besides the three Causeways —the Little, the Middle, and the Great—the "Lady's Fan," the "Organ," the largest and smallest pillars, and "Prince Arthur's Chair;" were given three sips of water from an old well, and then each of us made a wish while sitting in what is called the "Wishing Chair."

My wish really came true. I need not tell exactly what it was, but think a good guesser would come to the conclusion that it had something to do with letters from "the other side."

After buying books of views from an old woman eighty years old, and stopping for a moment to see a man put a white mouse into a cap, and shake out an Irish potato, we climbed into the car and drove back to Portrush. We had a splendid view of Dunluce Castle, the oldest ruin in Ireland. It is built on an island, and connected with the main-land by a natural bridge only eighteen inches wide.

While passing through Belfast in the afternoon we tried to get a glimpse of the rioters (called "patriots" in America), but every thing on our route was quiet and peaceful.

Crossing the Irish Sea on a boat called the "Grampus," we arrived at Glasgow, Scotland, about five o'clock in the morning. First, a good nap, followed by breakfast at half-past twelve, and we were ready for sight-seeing.

It was raining in the afternoon, so we took a cab and drove round the city. The residence streets were especially handsome, and the business thoroughfares, as dark came on, were quite brilliant with gas and electricity.

When we ladies rose from the dinner-table that evening every gentleman in the dining-room arose too, and remained standing until we had passed out. It was an act of courtesy we had never seen before, and impressed us favorably with Scotch manners.

As we actually had gas in our bed-rooms, we girls wanted to sit up nearly all night in order to enjoy the novelty of it. It was so cool that fires were pleasant necessities. The next day (Sunday) we started out to attend religious service, and I think even if we had not so intended would have drifted to church with the current, for the whole population seemed to be surging in great waves to the various places of worship.

We heard Dr. Burns preach, but his accent was so queer that it was difficult to understand him. The music was grand, and just before the service closed they sung a familiar hymn, in which we all joined heartily. It was a Presbyterian Church, of course, but the order of worship was not like that of the Presbyterians at home.

Many of the streets were so steep that walking was rather a climbing exercise. The street-cars had seats on top, with stairs to go up.

One morning we had Highland mutton and Scotch herring for breakfast. In the center of the table was "a dish fit for a king" to look upon—a bowl of beautiful Scotch heather.

CHAPTER IV.

TROSACHS—STIRLING—EDINBURGH.

LEAVING Glasgow Monday morning, we rode for a short distance along the banks of the Clyde, where a great deal of ship-building was going on. Many steamers were in the docks for repairs, and others were in process of construction.

Leaving the train at Balloch pier, we boarded a little steamer which carried us across Loch Lomond to Inversnaid, a distance of twenty-one miles.

From the lake there was a fine view of the rugged old mountain, Ben Lomond, of poetic fame. The scenery on all sides was beautiful —much like that of the Hudson River. We were welcomed on landing by the melodious strains of a bagpipe, the first we had heard on Scottish soil. On leaving the vessel we climbed into a long coach, or Tally-ho, and went dashing through the Trosachs in fine style. Several barefooted, little boy beggars followed our coach nearly all the way up the mountain, pleading for "a penny, gentlemen, please, sir, if you please," and to attract our attention threw bunches of heather into the carriage.

We spent half an hour at Stronaclacher, where Loch Katrine can be seen to the best advantage; and such a lovely little toy-lake as it is! Susie and I brought away with us some ferns and wild flowers that we gathered from near the edge of the water.

How delighted we were when our next steamer drew up to the pier and we found it to be the "Rob Roy," the tiniest thing to be called a *steamer* we had ever seen! Nevertheless, it carried us bravely across the loch, past the beautiful little isle of Ellen,* and on to the other side.

Entering another coach, we went whirling over the mountains again, only stopping long

---

*"Lady of the Lake."

enough at the Trosachs Hotel to get nicely warmed up with Scotch broth: so ravenously hungry was I that nothing ever tasted better. Our ride carried us past numerous small lochs, and over the "Brigg of Turk." We also had a fine view of Ben Venue and Benledi.

The spot where Rob Roy planted the fiery cross was pointed out, as was also the place where Roderick and Fitz James fought the duel. Leaving the coach at Callander, the train carried us to Stirling, where we were glad enough to rest our weary bodies and think over the delightful experiences of the day.

Starting out early next morning to see something of Stirling, we drove first to the castle. Stationed at the entrance were several sentinels dressed in the regular Highland costume—kilts, plaids, and all. They looked rather cool with such short skirts, and bare legs. Passing over the draw-bridge, we entered a winding passage and saw what is called the "Lion's Den;" also the room where James II. assassinated the Earl of Douglas. Then we had a magnificent view from the

EDINBURGH CASTLE.

ramparts, and sat on the step where Mary Queen of Scots once rested, and looked at the scenery through a small round opening in the wall.

Going down to the old Greyfriars' Church, built in 1494, we saw the place where James VI. was crowned, and where John Knox preached the coronation sermon; we then hurried to the station just in time to catch the train for Edinburgh.

Our hotel there was the Royal, on Prince's Street. Starting out sight-seeing almost immediately, we climbed up to the old castle, where they showed us a great many interesting relics. The regalia of Scotland dazzled our eyes with its magnificence. We entered Queen Mary's chamber, where James VI. was born—quite a small, plain-looking room—and then visited Margaret's chapel, the oldest building and the smallest chapel in Scotland.

We examined with great interest Mons Meg, the monster cannon which was burst in firing a salute upon some special occasion.

Holyrood Palace was our next stopping-place, and there we were shown the rooms of Lord Darnley and Queen Mary, with the same old furniture they used ranged round the walls. Such a funny old bed, such queer, slim chairs, and such faded coverings! We girls stole a peep at our bangs in the curious little mirror in Queen Mary's dressing-case.

They showed us the famous blood-stains on the floor, and then we went down and saw the ruins of the old abbey.

In the distance could be seen the Frith of Forth, tumbling and glistening in the sunlight.

Not far from our hotel, on Prince's Street, was the magnificent Scott monument, standing in a little park. Mary Green and I concluded to attempt the ascent; so up we toiled, up and up, until we could look down on eight-story houses. It seemed to me we would never reach the top, and the little winding stairs were so narrow and steep that I scratched my hands on the walls, and took every step in constant terror of tumbling back the next. We were fully rewarded, however, by the view from the summit, for the panorama of beautiful Edinburgh spread out before us was a sight worth climbing many steps to see.

Next day was spent at the Exposition, where there were so many wonderful things to be seen that a full description would be impossible.

There was a street arranged to represent Old Edinburgh, with all sorts of funny little stalls and booths, where they sold a variety of queer things. The shop-keepers were dressed in the styles of a hundred years ago, and spoke such a strange old Scotch dialect that even the Scotch people themselves could not understand the language, and laughed at it as much as we did.

Going back to our hotel we girls begged to be allowed to ride on top of the street-car, and, permission being granted, we clambered up and had fine fun from our elevated position.

We left Edinburgh next day, and reached Melrose by twelve o'clock. How we enjoyed the grand old abbey! such a quiet, restful place after the whirl and hurry of a great city! We examined the different chapels, the strange inscriptions, and the beautiful arches and pillars that have escaped destruction. Before the place where the high altar stood is a stone which covers a casket containing the heart of Robert Bruce, and on the right is the grave of Michael Scott, the wizard. I could not help wishing all the time that Oliver Cromwell and the rest of the destroyers had turned their attention to something else, and left the fine old abbey in its former beauty and splendor. It is really sad to see the ruin and devastation of those rude hands.

Next we drove out to Abbotsford, Scott's charming home. Having seen its beauty, I am not surprised that he loved it so much. They conducted us first into the great hall; next to his study, where this wonderful genius toiled for so many years; then through the library, drawing-room, and armory. On Sir Walter's desk was a box made of wood from the Spanish Armada, and beside it his well-worn chair. Among other curiosities scattered through the different rooms were Scott's last suit of clothes, his sword, purse, Burns's drinking-glass, Rob Roy's sword, a very beautiful ebony cabinet, fifteen chairs presented by George IV., and Queen Mary's jewelry-box, with the cross which she held when executed.

The gentle ripple of the Tweed came in at the library windows, and looking around we saw twenty thousand volumes collected by the great author. The paper on the walls of the drawing-room was very curious—being hand-painted, and supposed to have been the work of Chinese artists.

We drove back to Melrose, and lunched at the Abbey Hotel; then took the train for Appleby, which we found to be a sleepy little country town. We lodged at a regular old-fashioned English Inn, the King's Head, and the reader may be sure we enjoyed this new experience. Our dinner was served in a cheerful little coffee-room, all to ourselves, and we had the freshest butter, nicest honey, whitest bread, and the richest yellow cream we had seen since leaving Tennessee. It really tasted like a good **home-supper.**

We were up bright and early next morning, and took a long walk around the place before **the dew** was off the grass, filled our lungs with fresh country air, and felt prepared to plunge into all the smoke and fog that even London might have in store for **us.**

CHAPTER V.

LONDON.

A WHOLE day was consumed in making the trip from Appleby to London; consequently we were glad to reach the end of our journey, and secure nice rooms at the Inns of Court Hotel, which, as may be supposed from the name, has always been a favorite stopping-place for lawyers.

What great rejoicing there was next morning when Uncle Robert returned from Cook's office with our mail — the first since leaving home! Five letters, besides papers, fell to my share, and with a voracious appetite for news I immediately sat down to devour them. When every thing had been read, reread, and discussed, we started for a walk, passed down Fleet Street, and, being attracted to St. Paul's Cathedral by the chimes, were just in time for the evening service, and heard some very sweet music by fifty little choristers. Then we went over the church, and looked at the various monuments and inscriptions, which were of the usual type.

On going to our rooms at night it was customary to stop at a little table in the hall, and take with us one of the candles placed there. We girls discovered that here was a good opportunity to get more light, so occasionally we helped ourselves generously, and made a rush for our rooms in order to escape the vigilant eye of the chambermaid. However, this was only done when *dark* necessity compelled.

The weather was all we could have wished, and we had not a chance, as yet, to decide how we liked a London fog.

A very peaceful Sabbath was spent in attending service at St. Paul's in the morning, and driving home by the Parliament Houses, Westminster Abbey, Somerset House, along the Thames Embankment, and up Fleet Street and the Strand.

Next morning we started out sight-seeing in earnest, making Westminster Abbey our first stopping-place after having seen Charing Cross, Trafalgar Square, the old Bank of England, and many other interesting things and places. I shall leave to the guide-books and learned travelers an enumeration of all the tombs and monuments with which the old abbey is filled, and only add that we spent several hours wandering within its gloomy walls, and then managed to make our way out through the crowds which were constantly pouring in.

While waiting before the American Exchange who should come up but Misses Emma and Lillie Morrow, of Miss Ford's party—all of Nashville. They accepted an invitation to dine with us in the evening, and we had quite a pleasant time talking over our various experiences and the latest home news.

I was afraid that during our stay in London I would injure my eyes trying to look at both sides of the street at once, to say nothing of occasional glimpses before and behind.

As loyal Methodists, of course we visited City Road Chapel, and saw the house where John Wesley lived, his pulpit, desk, and chair.

We were allowed to gather as souvenirs some little sprigs of green from the grave of the great founder. Across from City Road is Bunhill Fields Cemetery, where, besides the graves of Bunyan, De Foe, and Isaac Watts, is that of Susanna, the mother of the Wesleys.

On Tuesday morning we took a long drive through Hyde Park to the Albert Memorial in Kensington Gardens. This monument is erected on the site of the first World's Fair. The lower part of it is beautiful, but the general effect is rather spoiled by the gilding and gaudy colors on its top. At the corners are marble pieces representing Europe, Asia, Africa, and America. These are finely executed, and if not presumptuous we would suggest that Victoria made a mistake in not having the whole monument constructed of white marble and ornamented with fewer glaring colors.

Driving along Piccadilly, we saw the Rothschild mansion and the houses of the Dukes of Devonshire and Cambridge. Among the palaces seen on that same morning were Buckingham, St. James, and the residences of the Prince of Wales and his brother, the Duke of Connaught, who was at that time absent in India.

The Queen was not at Buckingham; in fact, it was said that she rarely spent more than five days there during the year. The Prince of Wales was entertaining the King of Portugal at the royal palace.

Our next "lion" was the old Tower of London. Going first to the jewel-room, we feasted our eyes on the most magnificent regalia in the world. More conspicuous than any thing else was the crown, valued at £1,000,000. Placed all around this were the various orbs, diadems, maces, scepters, royal plate, and other beautiful works of art in gold and precious stones. We were shown a model of that great diamond, the Koh-i-noor—the original being worn in a brooch by the queen. I could have spent hours gazing at these glittering treasures, but we were obliged to make the most of our time, so passed on to the armory. Here were displayed all kinds of weapons, and many curious suits of armor from England, France, India, China, and numbers of different places. There was a figure on horseback which represented Queen Elizabeth as she appeared when on her way to St. Paul's to give thanks after the destruction of the great Armada. In the center of the court of the Tower was a brass tablet marking the spot where the scaffold stood on which Lady Jane Grey, Anne Boleyn, and Catherine Howard were beheaded. Coming down the narrow stairs, we passed the place where the two poor little princes were buried after having been so cruelly murdered.

That evening we met some very pleasant people in the drawing-room of the hotel. One young fellow, who had the appearance and pronunciation of a dude, joined in the conversation, and we were much amused at some of his remarks, which were invariably prefaced and punctuated with such decidedly English expressions as "awfully jolly," "awfully nice," "awfully narsty," "beastly," "darn't you knaw," and others of like character. He inquired if we were from Canada, and did not seem at all complimented when somebody asked if he were a *Frenchman*.

Wednesday we spent at the Japanese village, and a charming day it was. A whole colony of Japanese live there, working at their different trades, keeping house, and seemingly as contented and happy as if in their native country. They were dressed in the national costumes, and chatted merrily with each other in their own language. We watched the process of hair-dressing, which was very curious, and then walked around and bought some little straw boxes of Japanese sweets from a queer-looking old woman. We fell completely in love with two cunning little Japanese children, who trotted about on their tiny wooden shoes, and did not seem to be afraid of anybody. In a bamboo cage was a small Japanese dog with a turned-up nose. He was quite gentle, and kindly allowed us to pat him on the head as much as we liked. After attending two entertainments, and seeing some very wonderful umbrella feats, wire-walking, and screen-balancing, besides hearing some strange Japanese music, and watching some of the ladies go through with their native dances, we reluctantly took our leave. I think Mary Green really wanted to carry off one of those tiny Japs.

Next day we went shopping, and I am sure we must have walked many miles, for we did not get back to lunch until two o'clock.

One china-store that we visited was particularly beautiful. There was a very large room full of fine glass-ware of every description. The roof was of stained glass, and it seemed as though we had wandered into fairy-land. The walls were lined with mirrors, and the cut-glass chandeliers, which were suspended from the ceiling, were reflected and re-reflected in glittering splendor. Here and there twinkled little colored fairy-lights, and we scarcely dared to move for fear this dazzling, sparkling bubble which enveloped us would burst and leave only a little *soap* in our eyes.

After lunch we visited Madame Tussaud's wax-works. Here we found ourselves face to face with all the heroes and heroines of ancient and modern times—Napoleon Bonaparte, nearly all the kings and queens of England; Victoria, with her whole family, surrounded by her court; our own George Washington, Garfield, John Wesley, Byron, Burns, Shakespeare, and hundreds of others. We watched the life-like breathing of the sleeping beauty, and could hardly persuade ourselves that she was not alive. Uncle Robert walked up and put his hand on the shoulder of a policeman stationed near the door, and said something to him. Imagine his surprise when he found he had been talking to a man of wax!

Passing on to another room, Susie and I climbed into Napoleon's coach, and had its various conveniences explained to us. Then we went down into the Chamber of Horrors, and saw enough murderers, thieves, and other terrible characters to supply us with bad dreams for a whole month.

The next day was spent in the Zoological Garden, said to be the largest in the world. While standing before one of the monkey-cages Susie got too close, and in an instant one of the monkeys had reached out and snatched every particle of trimming from her hat, and, screaming with delight, went climbing up into the top of the cage with his prize streaming out behind him. Susie's face, when she discovered her loss, was a picture, and the little boys who were standing around fairly roared and shrieked with amusement. What fun those monkeys did have with that ribbon! They dressed up in it, fought over it, pulled it to pieces, and altogether had such a thoroughly good time that we told the keeper not to take it away from them, as he offered to do. Another amusing sight was watching "Old Sallie," the orang-outang, put on a kid glove. She knew just how to smooth down the fingers, and seemed to be intensely interested in having it fit exactly right. Before leaving we girls took a ride on a big elephant, also on a camel. I prefer the gait of the elephant. It does not jerk one quite so hard.

We had our courier, Mr. Dattari, an Italian from Florence, to dine with us that evening, and found him to be quite an elegant gentleman. His conversation was interesting, and he spoke good English.

We had by this time become very much at home in London, and found our way around to different places without any trouble whatever.

I wish I had time to tell of all the wonderful places visited and the people we met, but must hurry on, lest we tarry too long in the great metropolis.

CHAPTER VI.

FROM LONDON TO BRIGHTON.

ON Saturday we decided to make an excursion, selecting Sydenham as the most desirable place to visit. It was only a short ride from London, and the weather was fine. Leaving the train, we walked around the Crystal Palace for some time, looking at the statuary, fountains, beautiful tropical plants, works of art, and various fancy things in the booths. After lunch we went into the music-hall and heard a grand organ recital, then took our places before the stand and beheld the mysterious trick of the "vanishing lady." Some Japanese performers came on, and entertained us highly with their dexterous feats. Next on the programme were some wonderful aerial performances, which fairly made our heads swim.

By this time they were beginning to light up, and when the great building was fully illuminated with thousands and thousands of colored lights, it seemed an enchanted place, while the splashing of the fountains and the sounds of exquisite music did not dispel the illusion. We turned away with reluctance, deciding this to have been a day running over with pleasure.

Sunday was damp and rainy, but we went to church in spite of the weather—drove across the river to the Tabernacle to hear Spurgeon, one of the greatest preachers in the world, deliver one of his best sermons. I felt quite at home when the immense congregation of five thousand people sung a hymn to Duke Street without an organ, and every stanza lined. The second prayer was grand, followed by the sermon—plain and simple enough for any child to understand — perfectly practical, with no flowery flights, and so earnestly and forcibly delivered that, as Susie said, "You had to listen whether you wanted to or not." The minister did not have on a gown,—this was a great comfort to us and him—and he did not read his sermon.

Monday was spent at the British Museum, and the simple act of *seeing* was no light undertaking. We were interested in the ancient manuscripts, books in old type, and many other curious things; but I will be honest enough to confess that the broken-nosed, legless, armless, headless, and oftentimes bodiless pieces of statuary had little beauty or attraction for me; in fact, proved to be rather what our English friends would call "an awful bore, don't you know!" My taste very evidently needed cultivation in that direction.

Mr. Arthur Marks, of Tennessee, called on our party in the evening. Of course we were glad to meet somebody from home.

Next day we visited the National Art Gallery, and saw hundreds of the treasured works of the old masters. I was most pleased with Murillo's "Holy Family."

Then we went to the Kensington Museum and the Indian Exhibit, where there were more pictures, statues, old carriages, lovely china and porcelain, Indian ornaments, exquisite embroidery, beautiful brocades, Chinese pagodas, ivory boxes, carved chairs, queer-looking musical instruments, besides countless thousands of other things that I cannot remember.

Another excursion was planned for the next day, this time up to old York, in the north country. As we walked into the dining-room of the hotel in York that evening I heard a gentleman whisper: "They are Americans." I should like to know how he knew it, for I do not think we had even spoken.

As soon as breakfast was over next morning, we took an open carriage and drove around York—or rather into York, for our hotel was outside the walls of the old city proper. We saw the castle, many curious houses with projecting upper stories that almost met across the narrow streets, the Lord Mayor's mansion, and last, but not least, the old Minster, for which the place is famous. The "Five Sisters" window excited our admiration, and we spent an hour wandering about the church looking at its massive architecture and curious relics.

We then took the train for Cambridge, and

were driven over the town, saw its seventeen colleges—the principal one of which is **Trinity**, its beautiful grounds shaded with grand old English oaks—and reached the station just an hour too soon, the hungriest crowd in Great Britain. Uncle Robert was sent out on a foraging expedition, and came back with some sandwiches. These were soon devoured, and he went for more. Another supply disappeared as quickly as the first. The third time he returned with a bag of cold boiled eggs. We finished these and called for more. There were no more, so we ordered that some be cooked, and, as they were only just done when the train came, we got into the carriage and continued our feast on hot eggs instead of cold ones.

Reaching London rather late, we spent the night at the St. Pancras Hotel, which is said to be one of the finest in Europe.

A visit to the Indian and Colonial Exhibition occupied the next day, where much of interest was to be seen.

Old London was represented, and we drank

water from a fountain in one of its narrow streets. Wandering into the garden, we sat down to listen to the music, and asked a waiter for some lemonade. He brought us four bottles, and poured their contents into our glasses. It tasted something like hard cider, but more like inferior soda-water. We concluded that the *old* English did not know how to make good lemonade. One very interesting sight of the Exhibition was a perfect representation of an African jungle, with the tigers, lions, wild boars, monkeys, undergrowth, and all complete. We staid until after dark to see the grand illuminations. Just as the clock chimed the half-hour past six all the grounds burst into light. The tops of the buildings were outlined with tiny, twinkling globes; also the monuments, shrubs, trees, flower-beds, and every conceivable place that could hold a light. The whole was made more brilliant by electricity, while a fountain in the center of the lake sparkled and rippled with all the colors of the rainbow.

Susie and I decided to take a rest-day, so

on Saturday, while **Aunt Anna and Mary G.** went shopping, we remained at the hotel and spent the time reading, writing, practicing, and lounging.

On Sunday morning Dr. Parker preached at the City Temple. I was forcibly reminded, all during his discourse, of Henry Irving, the actor. Their voices were alike, and they had much the same manner and gestures. There was too much elocutionary effort in the sermon for me, and it contained very few striking thoughts, but was replete with pretty words.

As I was sealing a letter in our room that night, Mary G. rushed in and announced that Mr. and Mrs. Charles Eastman were downstairs. We hurried to the drawing-room, and sure enough there they were—had come over on the "Umbria," been through a storm, and landed at Liverpool the day before. They engaged rooms at the "Inns of Court," and at dinner next day we had the whole party assembled, with the addition of Miss Macklin, a young lady who came over on the steamer with Mr. and Mrs. Eastman.

We ladies spent the next day in going through Whitley's immense store. I could have squandered a large fortune there with but little effort, and could have furnished a whole house, from a pug-dog to a piano.

Next day we made an excursion up the Thames to Carlyle's house, No. 24 Cheyne Row, Chelsea, a very plain, unpretending domicile. Here the great author lived for nearly twenty-five years, and here also was the scene of poor Mrs. Carlyle's perplexing household cares. There were placards in the windows announcing that it was "to let." Then we went down the river past Somerset House, Lambeth Castle, and the Tower, under old London Bridge, past the docks and wharves, and on to Greenwich, to visit the Observatory. Just think of it! From there we rode back almost the whole way to our hotel, a distance of fifteen miles, on a street-car!

Another long rest-day, as the weather was bad, and we got on the train and ran down to Brighton. First we visited the Pavilion, which was occupied by Queen Victoria during her early married life. Then we went down to the beach and walked out to the end of the new chain-pier. The fishermen were there mending their sails, with nets spread on the sands to dry. Susie and I had "lots" of fun running races with the breakers. It was while walking along the chain-pier that Uncle Robert asked an old confectionery woman " which one of his daughters most resembled him?" Her answer was: "The two other young ladies look like their mother, but this one," pointing to me, "is *exactly* like her father, sir." We were much amused at the way she had tangled our relationship. After driving for some time along the beach, meeting numbers of handsome turn-outs, we turned our faces Londonward again, and that night marked down in our journals another red-letter day.

On Friday the clerk of the weather concluded to give us some variety, so we were favored with a genuine London fog. At half-past nine we ate breakfast by gas-light, and were obliged to light the candles in our rooms. Susie and I did not go out, and at twelve o'clock we could not see to read at the drawing-room windows without the gas, and all the street-lamps were lighted. I was glad to have seen a genuine London fog, but *one* was enough. The fog is of a peculiar color—a kind of greenish, grayish yellow—and seems almost thick enough to cut with a knife.

That night we girls had a feast in our room. We spread a towel over the table, made lemonade in the glasses on the wash-stand, and stirred it with the handles of our tooth-brushes. The chambermaid brought us some ice; we begged the sugar from one of the waiters; laid out our store of sweets—consisting of candy, apples, a pear, and a little butter-scotch—and secured enough extra candles to have a grand illumination. I heard one of the three complaining next morning that she did not feel very well, but the other two were all right.

The time for leaving England having drawn near, we began packing in earnest, as the trunks were to be left in London until our return eight months hence. Our valises were well stuffed, and it took a great deal of strapping and squeezing before we could close them.

On Sunday we rested, after hearing Dr. Shorr preach in a very energetic manner at the Wesleyan Chapel.

Next morning, when we started from the hotel, all the waiters, porters, chambermaids, "boots," and clerks that we had ever even looked at were assembled to see us off; and such smiles, bows, and farewells! We returned their adieus with *shillings*, and, giving ourselves entirely into our courier's charge, stepped into the waiting cabs, were driven to the station, and continued our journey to the far East. From this time forward we became "Cookies," as Cook's tourists are called in Europe, and surely nothing that could have been desired to make our trip comfortable and pleasant was left undone. We were relieved of all care and responsibility, our mail was forwarded regularly and safely, and the whole burden of travel made as easy and delightful as possible.

CHAPTER VII.

PARIS.

ON the way from London to Dover we passed through Canterbury, famous for its cathedral, where Thomas à Becket was murdered in 1170, and also for the association of the quaint old tales of Chaucer.

We had been dreading the crossing of the English Channel, and it was with fear and trembling that we stepped on board the "Petrel." However, the sky was blue, the water calm, and every thing so charming, that our little vessel proved not to be a "stormy petrel," and carried us across as gently and smoothly as could have been desired. Nobody was seasick except Susie, and she had only a slight attack.

As soon as a landing was made at Calais, what a jabbering and confusion greeted our ears! The porters were shouting and yelling in French, and I realized forcibly, for the first time, that I was "a stranger in a strange land."

Another long journey on the train, a farcical examination of the baggage, and we were at last in beautiful Paris, rattling along its brilliantly lighted streets in cabs.

None of our party spoke any of the foreign languages, so we left all the arrangements about rooms, etc., to our courier, Mr. Dattari, and he proved himself thoroughly competent to take care of us.

I could have slept till noon the next day, if Uncle Robert had not waked us early, in order to make ready and start out sight-seeing.

It seemed strange not to be able to read the signs and advertisements, and not to understand what the people were saying as they passed us on the streets.

Of course we went first to the Palace of the Louvre, which is a great museum of beautiful things of art. A great many copyists were at work before the grand old masterpieces of painting, and some of their efforts were fine. The decorations of the walls and ceilings of the palace were magnificent, and the great glittering halls stretched out in seemingly endless perspective. One very attractive feature was a set of thirty immense paintings by Murillo, representing different scenes in the life of Maria de' Medici. We came out tired and hungry, and glad to find a cake-shop where lunch could be obtained.

On our return to the hotel in the afternoon, we lost our way for a little while, but it did not take long to find it again.

At the St. Petersburg Hotel, where we were stopping, the dining-room ceiling was made of glass, and several evenings at dinner we thought we heard it raining. Finally, concluding it was a little peculiar that it should rain every day just at that time, we investigated and discovered that the water was from an artificial fountain, arranged so as to trickle on the glass roof, and that our rain was counterfeit; but it was pleasant music to eat by, for all that.

We found in Paris one of our Nashville young ladies, Miss Nannie Seawell, who had also come over on the "Umbria" with Mr. and Mrs. Eastman. She was studying art, and was very much interested in her work. She and Mrs. Trezevant called on our party at the hotel once or twice.

We joined one of Cook's excursion parties, and rode around the city in an immense wagon or stage, large enough to accommodate twenty-five or thirty persons. We had a regular *valet de place* to point out objects and buildings of note, and saw so much to interest and entertain us that it would be impossible to tell the half of it; so I will simply mention a few of the most prominent places visited, without attempting minute descriptions of any.

First we passed the Place and Column Vendome. This old column was made of cannon captured in war by the French. Then we went down the Rue de Rivoli, a fine arcaded street, passed the gardens of the Tuileries, to the mint, and into the beautiful little Sainte

Chapelle, where is some of the richest and most gorgeous stained glass in the world.

We were conducted up into the Palace of Justice, and to the Louvre again, where we noticed a great many things we had missed the day before, among them the statuary and royal apartments. The Venus de Milo of course attracts a great deal of attention here; but, to be honest, I did not admire the face or form of this celebrated statue as much as I did some of the others, which may have been the result, on my part, of an uncultivated taste.

Lunching at a little hotel near by, we had wine for the first time; but I do not think the party, as a whole, enjoyed it. After visiting St. Sulpice Church, we went to the Luxembourg Gallery. It is here that the works of modern artists are shown, and some of us agreed that the "new masters" had, according to our judgment, improved in many respects upon the old ones. Next we were shown the Gobelin tapestry, and even the gentlemen of our party went into ecstasies over its beauty.

It was all done by hand, from the wrong or under side, and could not be distinguished from the most exquisite oil paintings unless examined closely. I would not have believed that any thing made of threads could have been so beautiful. None of the work is for sale, but is owned by the Government, and only given away as royal presents.

We were conducted through the Pantheon, where **Victor Hugo, Voltaire, and other** great **literary** men and unbelievers are buried, visited the handsome church of St. Steven, and then went (O horrors!) to the Morgue. There were two bodies exposed, both old men. The sight was so revolting that we left as quickly as possible, fervently hoping we would not dream of suicides.

Our sight-seeing for that day was ended by a visit to the grand Cathedral of Notre Dame. It would be folly for me to attempt a description of this celebrated building, so I will pass it by without comment, as a "tale that has been (often) told."

One morning, while we were at breakfast,

a colored lady and gentleman of "African descent" walked into the dining-room and placed themselves at one of the tables near us. They remained at the hotel several days, and we saw them often on the streets, driving around in a stylish turn-out, behind a pair of spirited horses, with a white driver. They were from the Gold Coast of Africa, and spoke both English and French fluently.

Our rooms were very nicely furnished, with large mirrors over the mantels and in the wardrobes, pretty lace curtains at the windows and over the beds, with handsome brass clocks in each apartment; but alas! no soap. Fortunately, we were supplied, so it did not matter.

The working-men looked very queer with long blue frocks exactly like shirts, worn in the place of coats, while the women sported peculiar-looking bonnets or head-dresses; the costumes of the *bonnes,* or nurse-maids, were quite picturesque, with flowing ribbons, long cloaks, and snow-white aprons.

The second day's excursion carried us first to the Church of the Madeleine; but as preparations were being made for a funeral we could not enter the building.

The Place de la Concorde and the Obelisk of Luxor were interesting, as were also the Champs Elysees and the Palace of Industry.

TOMB OF NAPOLEON.

We viewed the panorama of the battle of Champigny, and then passed the grandest triumphal arch in the world, that of Napoleon I.

Entering the Palace of Trocadero, we climbed into the tower, from which elevation we had a very fine view of Paris, making the descent on the largest "lift," or elevator, in the world—Edoux's.

We were delighted with the splendor of Napoleon's tomb, and went through Hotel des Invalides, which has accommodations for six thousand soldiers, though occupied by only three hundred and thirty at the time of our visit.

After lunching at one of the restaurants in the Palais Royal, we visited the Church St. Eustache, saw the Halles Centrales, the Boulevard de Sebastopol, Place and Statue de la Republique, and halted before the Column of July, which marks the place where the old Bastile, of so many terrible associations, once stood. The column is very high, and on top is a figure of Liberty.

Walking through the celebrated cemetery, Pere la Chaise, we gathered a pebble from the grave of Abelard and Heloise, and some ivy-leaves from the tombs of Marshal Ney and Racine.

Passing on through the poorer quarters of

Paris, we reached the **Park** of Buttes Chaumont, a charming place; crossed a rather shaky **little supension** bridge, and had a beautiful view of the lake. As we drove off some one in the *cafe* played on the piano, "God Save the Queen," and then "Yankee Doodle." The latter was greeted with applause from the Americans, while some of us would not have objected to a rendition of "Dixie."

We also passed the residence of President Grevy, and a very beautiful place it was. In front of all the *cafe's*, out on the pavements, were small tables and chairs, where **in pleasant weather great numbers of** people sat, eating **ices, drinking wine and coffee,** while engaged in most animated conversation.

Starting out on Friday to take our third **excursion, we found a five-in-hand** awaiting us, and, although it **was** raining, our party numbered fifteen. **After passing the Church of St. Augustine,** we drove through the Bois de Boulogne, which contains seven artificial lakes, a lovely cascade, and several very fine avenues.

Mary Green and I were the only ones of our seven who cared to walk through the town of St. Cloud, but we felt fully repaid after seeing the park and ruins of the old palace which was occupied by the French kings and queens from 1500 to 1870, when it was destroyed by the Communists. The old fountains were still beautiful, and we brought way with us from beneath the trees some buckeyes, "for luck."

Meeting the carriage on the opposite side of the park, we drove to the Grand Trianon, built by Louis XIV. for Madame de Maintenon. Here we were shown the private apartments of Napoleon and Josephine, also the rooms prepared for Queen Victoria when she spent a night there. They were all very magnificent, and full of rare and costly articles.

Instead of taking a regular lunch we decided to purchase some fruit, so stepped into a shop where were displayed some fine pears. The shop-keeper could not speak English, and we did not understand French, so had to point and gesticulate very energetically before we could make ourselves understood. Finally, though, we learned the price, procured the fruit, paid for it, and left in triumph.

In the afternoon we had quite a pleasant trip out to Versailles, the grandest palace in the world. The grounds were superb, and we wandered around them for some time lost in wonder and admiration. There were ten thousand statues and one hundred and sixty-three fountains, all of which were kept in perfect order. It costs about $200,000 for the fountains to play three-quarters of an hour, so, as might be supposed, there is not more than one day in the year when they can be seen in all their splendor. The royal apartments were magnificent beyond description.

A lace spread on the bed of **Louis XIV.** was made by the ladies of France, and valued at several millions of francs. (A franc is about twenty cents of our money).

The grand ball-room was gorgeous, the walls being covered with immense mirrors, the ceiling exquisitely painted, and the floor waxed to such a degree that walking on it was rather a precarious exercise.

On the way back to the city we stopped at the famous Sevres porcelain-manufactory. In the show-rooms was a quantity of handsome ware, among other things several vases valued at more than thirty thousand francs. We noticed copies in porcelain of a great many of the fine paintings we had seen in the Louvre.

On our return Mary G. and I sat on the seat with the driver, and felt very high up in the world, being almost on a level with the second stories of the houses. As we passed along the children on the pavement cried out: "Vive l'Amerique!" How did they know we were Americans?

We afterward went into the Grand Opera House, the most magnificent one in the world, I suppose. Its beauty and splendor are far beyond my powers of description, and must be seen to be appreciated.

Saturday we ladies spent the day shopping at the Bon Marche, and were a tired company when the experience was over.

Sunday morning there was service at the Madeleine, and such performances I had never seen in a church before! The priests were dressed like circus-performers; some with white gowns and red skirts, others with red gowns, a few with yellow stripes down their backs, and still others all in white. They marched around, swinging incense, chanting, and carrying lighted candles. Of course it was all strange and even foolish to us, but the music was fine, and we enjoyed it greatly.

The next two days were spent shopping in the Magazin du Louvre, the shops of the Palais Royal, at the Bon Marche, up and down the Rue de Rivoli, and in various parts of the city. We found a great many pretty novelties in the shops, besides meeting with an occasional amusing experience. At one place we attempted to trade with a jolly-looking old Frenchwoman who could not speak a word of English, but were compelled to leave after vainly attempting to make her understand that we wanted a certain pair of lorgnettes, set a certain way, and to be ready on a certain day. She finally gave it up, and so did we, and left her shaking her fat sides with laughter.

I felt very proud one day at dinner when I asked the waiter in French for some sugar, and he actually understood and brought it to me. That was the first time I had tried to speak the language.

Our last impressions of Paris were more pleasant than the first, as the weather was more propitious, and we were only persuaded to make preparations for departure by the promise of a return and a longer stay next time.

CHAPTER VIII.

MARSEILLES—MEDITERRANEAN SEA.

FROM Paris to Marseilles was an all-night's journey, and our party of seven found the little compartment in the train rather crowded, as it was intended for only eight persons, while our hand baggage occupied the space of at least two.

After we had been in the coupe several hours Uncle Robert, who had been asleep, awoke suddenly, suffering from thirst. There was no water within reach, and he determined, when we stopped at the next station, to get out and find some. We all begged him not to risk it, as the train only waited three minutes, and there was danger of his being left. Some of us even laid violent hands on the skirts of his coat to keep him in; but all to no purpose. He was frantic from thirst, and rushed out, demanding of the Frenchmen standing by: "Water! I want some water, I *must* have some water!" They had no idea what he meant, and the case was becoming desperate, when, fortunately, a man who understood English passed by, appreciated the state of affairs, and brought him a glass of water just before the train moved off. It was one of the most amusing scenes I ever witnessed, and we laughed until we were tired at his energetic efforts to satisfy his thirst.

After passing through some beautiful portions of Southern France and enjoying the glimpses of fine scenery from the car windows we reached the hotel at Marseilles at 11 A.M.

As soon as we had removed the dust and dirt of travel, taken our lunch, and rested a little we entered an omnibus and rode to Notre Dame Church, which stands on quite an eminence just outside the city. Our vehicle was drawn by three horses driven tandem, while a little boy ran along to whip the front one as we ascended the hill.

The drivers made a very peculiar sound when they wanted their horses to go faster, and we girls amused ourselves trying to imitate them.

A number of beggars followed us all the way up, pleading most piteously for sous.

After admiring the cathedral, which is a fine building, but interesting principally from its historical associations, being built, it is said, on the site of an ancient temple of Diana, we enjoyed a magnificent view of the city, spread out below us, and reaching down to the shores of the "beautiful blue Mediterranean."

On the way back to the hotel we passed through the flower-market, and I bought a large bunch of tuberoses and violets for three sous (three cents). We had by this time learned the English and French money systems thoroughly, though I always had to translate the price of an article into dollars and cents before I could tell its real value.

We spent two days in Marseilles; but during that short time saw much that interested and entertained us. It is a queer old city, with a strange and quaint population. The houses nearly all have tiled roofs, and the people seem to live mostly in the open air. Many of the streets have two rows of trees down the middle, with a shady walk between and drives on either side for vehicles.

Our hotel was one of the finest we had seen, the dining-saloon being especially handsome. We feasted on delicious grapes, and tried fresh figs, but one taste of the latter was sufficient for us.

On Thursday morning all the baggage, steamer chairs, rugs, etc., were carried down to the "Sindh," where we soon followed, entertaining ourselves while waiting for the vessel to start by watching the bustling, hurrying crowd on the wharf. We had no friends to bid good-by, so spent the time observing the farewells of the other passengers. The ship was crowded, every berth being taken. I was surprised to see so many people on their way to Egypt.

We soon had our luggage arranged in the state-rooms, and "went to housekeeping" for the voyage.

The wind blew quite fiercely all day, and

the steamer rolled and tossed so violently that at dinner the cases for the dishes had to be put on the table.

Susie and I staid up on the deck for a long time, watching Mr. Dattari, who was trying to promenade up and down in spite of the pitching of the vessel.

We had as yet no thought of being seasick; however, when we sat down to the table a little later and tried to eat, the commotion became a *personal matter*, and we beat an ignominious retreat to our state-rooms. How old Neptune did tumble us about that night! I never realized before what it was to be a foot-ball.

The weather next morning was lovely, and we began to feel that there was yet some small pleasure left in life. There were a number of children on board, and it seemed strange to hear the little "tots" jabbering to each other in French. None of the servants or officers spoke English, and I do not know how we could have managed without our courier to interpret for us.

At night we entertained ourselves with music, and sometimes quite a little audience would gather round as we sung one of the familiar home-tunes, or some of the jolly negro melodies. The latter pleased Mr. Dattari especially, as he had never heard them before; and he would ask again and again for "Down by the River" and "Reeling on a Rock." We did not dare sing "Home, Sweet Home," but came out strong on "America."

There were two Sisters of Charity on board, and a couple of priests in robes, who were continually walking up and down the deck telling their beads and repeating their prayers.

My seat at the table was next to the leading opera singer at Cairo. She tried to converse with me, but as I could not understand her French, nor she my English, we had to give it up.

On Saturday we passed through the Strait of Messina, and had a good view of Italy on one side and Sicily on the other, with glimpses of Ætna and Stromboli.

One of the passengers—Dr. Pierce, of Baltimore—was very ill for some days, and everybody thought he was going to die. He was not only seasick, but had other serious trouble. Our whole hearts went out in sympathy to him, as he was alone so far away from home. Uncle Robert did all he could for him, and we were rejoiced at last to hear he was better.

On Sunday there was no service in the saloon, so the time was spent in reading, talking, and singing.

One evening the sailors, who were off duty, got up what they called a *caravan*, and a funny show it was. First came a curious kind of animal ringing a bell; then an Arab on a rickety-looking camel; next, what we took to be an ostrich, and after it a giraffe. An accordion, a drum, a bell, and a pair of cymbals furnished the music, while the beasts themselves howled, squealed, roared, shrieked, growled, and bellowed. Altogether it was a most amusing spectacle, and the little boys on board were wild with delight.

We met some very pleasant English people among the passengers, and the last day of the voyage one of the young gentlemen told our fortunes. He was very kind in his prognostications, and gave us no cause for complaint as to what the future might have in store for us.

Early on Tuesday morning we awoke and saw through our port-holes the light-house on the coast of Egypt. How delighted we were to see land again, and what rapid packing we did so as to hurry up on deck!

The trip had lasted five days and a half, and we were quite willing to leave the steamer and venture forth to see and enjoy the sights of this strange land.

CHAPTER IX.

ALEXANDRIA.

AFTER passing through two harbors, the steamer anchored just outside of Alexandria; and, as soon as the police had come on board, up came the Arabs like cats over the sides of the vessel, and such confusion cannot be imagined. They were dressed in all sorts of costumes, made in various ways and representing all the colors of the rainbow. Their trousers were so loose and baggy that they looked like skirts, and on their heads were either gorgeous turbans or the regular red fez with long black tassels. They climbed into and spread over the ship like a lot of chattering monkeys, screaming, quarreling, fighting, pushing one another's boats, and each trying to make a greater racket than his neighbor. It was by far the most exciting scene I ever witnessed, and by its novelty and *noise* made an impression that yet remains.

Cook's boat was in waiting with our boatmen and dragoman, and they rowed us ashore. We were glad to step on firm ground once more, though it was a whole day before we were entirely free from the rolling motion of the vessel.

Our party was conducted in open carriages to the hotel, the Khedevial, where the landlady handed to Aunt Anna a bunch of beautiful roses. It is a very pretty and ancient custom of theirs to present flowers to a guest on entering the house. We divided the bouquet, and wore it to breakfast. Some one on the steamer had remarked that we were "approaching a country where every thing smells but the flowers." The first part of this assertion we were easily induced to believe before reaching the hotel; but one whiff of those delicious roses was enough to disprove the slur contained in the latter part.

Our rooms were large, airy, and cool, with lofty ceilings, high windows, and neat, white beds, each canopied with dainty lace and snowy curtains. Our windows looked out on the garden or yard of the hotel; and, if my arms had been just a little longer, I could have gathered ripe dates from the palm-trees nodding their heads almost within the room. There were bananas hanging on the trees, and the most beautiful jessamines, roses, and other flowers blooming in great profusion along the walks.

After a light lunch of fruits, and a refreshing nap, we dressed and went down to the eight o'clock dinner, which was well served and greatly enjoyed. It was here that I tried for the first time my favorite fruit—dates, *fresh* and delicious, just gathered, and having rather a different flavor from the pressed fruit which we get in America. The rest of the party did not share my appreciation, so passed the dish over to me, and I left it almost empty. The last course was Egyptian coffee—a delightful beverage, served in tiny cups not much larger than a thimble.

Just after the fruit was put on the table

candles were brought in and set before the gentlemen, who lighted their cigarettes and puffed away very comfortably before leaving their seats. The waiters were Arabs dressed in the native costume; and there were so many strange things to see and get accustomed to about the hotel that we were kept continually interested and entertained.

After dinner Mrs. Eastman and Aunt Anna took a walk, bringing back with them some Egyptian candy, which was very good, tasting something like our taffy, but covered over with small seeds or nuts, which had a strange but pleasant flavor.

While in the drawing-room we heard quite a commotion out on the street. On going to the door we found it was caused by a procession of pilgrims returning from Mecca. They were women, and therefore rode in closed carriages. A band was playing, and a great many of the Arabs were carrying torches, and fairly making night hideous with their howling and shrieking.

Susie and I found a good piano, and spent

a delightful evening practicing duets, and some of our old pieces—that is, as many as we could remember without notes. We discovered that Mr. Dattari was quite a musician, and his playing contributed much to the pleasure of the evenings. He was also very intelligent, conversed well, and was full of fun, exerting himself in every possible way to add to our enjoyment.

After breakfast next morning we drove in open carriages out to Pompey's Pillar. Our courier had intended going with us, for although he had been in Alexandria frequently—and in fact lived there for awhile—he had never visited this celebrated old monument, which was such a wonder to us. Business prevented his going even this time, so we went under the care of the dragoman, Calipha, whose duty it was to conduct us about and act as regular guide.

The sun was very hot, but the Arabs were lying around on the pavements, streets, anywhere and everywhere, fast asleep, and evidently enjoying the heat.

Pompey's Pillar was a rough-looking old column of some kind of brownish-gray granite. We brought away several pieces of stone like the material of the monument, which we bought of the Arabs.

The beggars were so numerous and annoying that our dragoman had to beat them back with a stick, as they really seemed about to press up and catch hold of us in their earnest demands for money. A little baby in its mother's arms that could only speak one word would hold out its tiny hand and piteously wail: "*Backsheesh!*"

Next we visited a Mohammedan cemetery, where the bodies were all buried in a standing position, with their faces toward the east. The monuments were very peculiar, and altogether it was a dreary, desolate place.

After driving through the grounds of the khedive's palace we walked through several of the bazaars, and Mr. Eastman bought him a fez, which was pronounced very becoming.

After lunch and a good rest we took a drive out to the garden of a rich Greek named Antoniades, where a great many beautiful flowers and shrubs we had never seen before were kept fresh and green by means of irrigation. We met the owner of the garden taking a walk; our dragoman introduced us, and through his interpretation we had quite a pleasant little chat.

It was cool and bracing in Alexandria after sundown, and we enjoyed very much the drive along the canal on our return to the city.

Just at six o'clock all true Mohammedans say their prayers, and we saw a man out on the road drop down on his knees with his face toward Mecca, and go through with his devotions.

Having about exhausted the sights of this our first Oriental city, we packed the valises and made ready to leave, with the unanimous conclusion that this part of our trip was almost as strange and wonderful as being transported bodily into the midst of some marvelous scene of the "Arabian Nights."

CHAPTER X.

CAIRO—PYRAMIDS.

FROM Alexandria to Cairo was a hot, disagreeable trip. The dust poured in upon us; our hair and clothes soon changed color, and at several stations we were obliged to get out of the car and use the clothes-brush most energetically.

We lunched on the train, and reached our destination at about two o'clock in the afternoon, realizing then as we had never before the blessings of a good bath and plenty of ice-water, especially when we remembered that it was fresh from the mysterious Nile.

The scene at the station was quite an exciting one, as we elbowed our way through a crowd of noisy Arabs. There were several men—policemen, evidently—carrying whips, which they did not hesitate to use on the rabble.

We stopped at Shepheard's Hotel, where every thing was delightfully arranged, the broad stone veranda in front being especially pleasant, as from it could be seen the never-ending panorama of the streets, on which something novel and interesting was always going on.

After dinner we went for a walk, and such queer sights and sounds as greeted us on every side! At one place we passed a hall where a man was telling stories to a company of people, as in the "Arabian Nights." I think we would have stopped to listen if there had been the least chance of understanding what was said.

We found at the hotel two of our steamer acquaintances, Sir Edward and Lady Lechmere, an English baronet and his wife, who were in Egypt looking after a hospital for the blind, which they had established.

The first thing next morning was a visit to the old Mosque of Cairo. It was the dirtiest, most dilapidated building imaginable, but we were not permitted to enter until we had put on straw sandals provided for the purpose, as the sole of the shoe is considered unclean.

In spite of the sacredness of the place it was very amusing to see our efforts to walk in these slippers. Mine were large enough for a grown man, and I could not step very high without losing one, so was compelled to *slide* most of the time.

Next we visited the Grand Mosque, erected by Mehemet Ali, who is buried in the building. It was very handsome, the walls being lined with pure alabaster, the ceiling hung with crystal lamps burning richly-scented oil, and the floor spread with gorgeous Persian rugs. A number of devotees were there bowing their heads to the ground, and going through various forms required by their mode of worship. We bought, as souvenirs, some little pieces of alabaster like the material of the inside walls.

Then we went through old Cairo, where most of the Arabs live. Comparatively speaking, I had never seen dirt, poverty, and wretchedness before.

We had quite a picturesque-looking dragoman to conduct us around. His name was Abrahim, and he dressed in gorgeous Turkish suits, sporting a different one every day; long, baggy trousers of some colored silk material, a gay little embroidered jacket, the regulation fez, soft slippers turned up at the toes, and over all, which eclipsed all, an ordinary European overcoat!

In the afternoon we went to see the "howling dervishes." I never before heard such a dreadful din. They ranted and shrieked, swaying their bodies back and forth, gradually increasing the motion until exhausted. A cage of wild beasts could not have excelled them in vocal effort. Strange that any human being could imagine such performances to be divine worship!

Before entering the room Abrahim warned us not even to smile, as it would offend them greatly; and of course we were careful. One man played on a thundering sort of tambourine, while all the rest—about thirty—howled and danced. At the upper windows could be seen the poor women peeping in—not being allowed to come inside during the service.

Leaving these lunatics, we crossed over the Nile in a little boat to the Island of Rhoda, and were shown the place where Moses was found in the bulrushes. We also went into a Coptic Church, said to have been built on the spot where the Holy Family lived while in Egypt.

From the Citadel we had a fine view of Cairo, and in the distance ten of the pyramids and the river Nile.

We drove for some time along the fashionable promenade, but as most of the *nobs* had gone to the races only a few of them were visible.

We visited an Arabic school where the pupils sat round on the floor, all jabbering at the same time, while the old, *blind* teacher heard each one spell in turn. They were dirty little fellows, dressed in a single garment, but seemed to be as full of mischief as the better-clad boys in our own American schools. One bright little urchin with big black eyes handed

SCENE ON THE NILE.

us a spelling-book and then read for us in Arabic. As we passed out through the hall, which was a sort of cellar—the school-room being a basement-room—we were assailed on all sides by the small beggars shouting, "*Backsheesh, backsheesh!*" a cry that we were destined to hear many times before leaving this land of ruins, idleness, and idlers.

Saturday had been selected for our trip to the Pyramids, so early in the morning we were ready and eager to start. We four young people were in one carriage, with the married couples in another, and the drive was delightful. The road was cool and shady, with trees meeting across nearly all the way, only the wind was a little chilly.

Some English troops were to go into camp near the Pyramids, and we overtook thousands of them (for they moved very slowly) all marching in the same direction as our party. There were infantry and cavalry, also artillery on the backs of camels. We would have had trouble in passing them if it had not been for the kindness of Captain Lewis, of the "Buffs," one of our fellow-passengers on the "Sindh," who sent a runner ahead and had the way cleared for us; otherwise we would have been obliged to turn back and postpone the trip until some other day.

The great stone masses were in full view long before we came to them, and we girls were incredulous when Mr. Dattari informed us that there was still an hour's ride before reaching the base. It seemed only a few hundred yards away. We found, however, that he was correct.

I was much surprised, upon a near approach, to find the pyramids all rough and jagged; great rock steps, four or five feet high, and the surface broken and rugged in many places.

All of us except Uncle Robert and Aunt Anna ascended as far as the first opening, and it took two Arabs to push and one to pull each of us up.

We girls were wild to climb to the top, as we had gotten along so nicely thus far; but the wiser heads thought it not prudent, so we reluctantly came down. However, we had been up high enough to feel the "inspiration of elevation." Mr. Dattari went to the top in our stead, and waved his handkerchief from the summit, looking like a tiny pigmy "flourishing a postage-stamp."

Think of the base of the great Cheops covering *thirteen acres*, with height corresponding, and you can form some idea of its immense size.

THE SPHINX.

We walked over to the Sphinx, and went down into a temple containing some huge blocks of granite. The sand was quite tiresome to wade through, and we were hot and tired by the time the lunching-place was reached.

Mrs. Eastman rode on a donkey, and was escorted by Dr. Mahmoud, of the tribe of Bedouins who live about the Pyramids, while the sheik gravely escorted Aunt Anna. Mr. Dattari came to our assistance when needed, and the gentlemen took care of themselves.

We sat quite awed for some time beneath the quiet gaze of the grand and silent Sphinx. I cannot imagine any thing more majestic than the solemn expression of that stony face, the eyes looking out into space, calm and patient, watching still as they have been watching for so many centuries past.

Workmen had been excavating around the lower part of the Sphinx, and much more of it was visible than is usually shown in the pictures — the paws, breast, and shoulders being above ground. There is space enough between the forefeet to build a temple, while the body stretches out to the length of more than one hundred and forty feet.

We lunched in a little building erected for the use of the Prince of Wales when he visited there. Freshly-made Arabic coffee, cold meats, rolls, fruits, nuts, and all sorts of dainties were served, besides a quantity of dates which had been kindly provided for me.

In the afternoon we returned to Cairo, and visited the Boulack Museum, where are *lots* of old things dug up from the ruins—such as mummies, statues, coins, and curios of various kinds. We saw the mummy of Rameses II., which had been recently excavated.

Then we went down to the river to see a dahabeah, and boarded one of Cook's new Nile steamers—a very neat, trim little craft.

Mr. Dattari showed us a boat that was wrecked during the expedition under Chinese Gordon, he being on board at the time.

That evening we had some "Turkish delight," a kind of candy that tasted something like our marsh mallow drops; also a large bunch of superb roses, and quantities of white star jessamine of delicious fragrance.

You will be surprised to hear that the best

fare we found anywhere and the most beautifully served was right there in Cairo. The waiters dressed in rich Oriental costumes; the cooking was French, and some of the dishes so artistically ornamented that it seemed a pity to cut into them.

The water was kept cool in long-necked earthen jars, and tasted better than any we had drank elsewhere; in fact, every thing was charmingly arranged, and nothing left undone that would contribute to the comfort and convenience of the guests.

CHAPTER XI.

HELIOPOLIS—CAIRO.

AS there was no service to attend on Sunday, we drove out to Heliopolis, the site of the ancient Temple of the Sun, and the place where Moses was educated.

We assembled at the foot of the only remaining obelisk, and Uncle Robert gave a short but very instructive lecture on the history of the place. From here the "Needle" was sent that is now in Central Park, New York; also those in London, Paris, Berlin, and Rome.

We stopped at the Virgin's Tree, beneath the shade of which the Holy Family is said to have rested on their journey to Egypt.

They gave us some very pretty bunches of flowers from the little garden near by, and we had quite a lively time hopping out of the way of the small lizards, which were running around in the sun over the gravel walks.

We waded through the sand to an ostrich-farm, and found it quite an interesting place. There were ostriches of all sizes, and the eggs were as large as our heads. We saw some of the feathers after they had been dressed, also those in their natural state on the bird. From a little observatory on the farm we could look far out across the desert and see the place where the children of Israel passed on their journey to the "promised land."

Returning to the hotel, in the afternoon we saw the khedive pass by. I brought my glasses to bear upon him, and had a good look at his face. His complexion was quite dark, and he was dressed in a black suit with red fez, and rode in an open carriage attended by sixteen horse-guards. In front of the vehicle ran the two *sais*, who always precede the carriages of rich and titled people. They were picturesque-looking Arabs, and carried short wands in their hands. They ran along in front of the fleet Arabian horses as lightly and easily as if they had wings.

Mr. Dattari gave each of us a little curiosity

that he had obtained on one of his trips up the Nile. Mine was a ring of some dark-looking metal, with a blue stone in it, which came off the finger of a *real* mummy. The others were curious little idols and images.

Next day we went shopping in the bazaars. The dragoman went with us to do the bargaining, and sometimes I was really afraid he and the shop-keeper would come to blows in their excitement and eagerness to *jew* each other.

At the scent-bazaar we bought some attar of roses, and then looked at silks, carpets, slippers, brass, and many beautiful things. The dragoman never allowed us to pay more than half the price first asked for an article, as the salesman invariably left at least that much margin for falling.

Some of the streets, or passages, were very narrow, and the shops so small that the dealer could sit in the middle of the floor and reach most of his goods which were piled around on the shelves.

It seemed so queer to go shopping and do our trading sitting on the counter swinging

ONE OF OUR DONKEYS.

our feet over into the street; but that was really the way we did, as the floor of the shop was the only counter and situated immediately on the thoroughfares.

Very often we had to press close up against the wall in order to let the clumsy camels pass by, and a great many times actually caught hold of the sleepy little donkeys and pushed them out of our way.

After lunch we had a juggler perform for us on the veranda. He was very clever, and did many wonderful tricks. Next we visited the China-bazaar, and the shop-keeper served us with Arabic coffee between the bargains.

On the way back we stopped at the garden of Esbikiah, heard some queer Egyptian music, and saw a banyan-tree, which was a small forest in itself, and looked much as represented in pictures of it we had seen.

That night all of us except Uncle Robert and Aunt Anna went out on a regular "lark" —a donkey-ride by moonlight—and what a jolly time we did have! It was not quite as awe-inspiring an experience as the sight of the

Sphinx or Pyramids, but was equally enjoyable, combining as it did the ludicrous and the serious, the latter quality being confined exclusively to the donkeys. My donkey was the smallest of the number, but what he lacked in size he made up in spirit and pluck, managing to keep to the front most of the time.

Each lady had a little donkey-boy to run along and *beat*, at times assisting the progress of his steed by a vigorous twist of the tail. The bridles were covered with bangles, or bells, and our cavalcade kept up a merry jingling as we dashed along the quiet road by the side of the Nile, with the moon peeping at us through the tall, shadowy palm-trees, its light beautifully reflected from the shining water below.

My donkey's name was "Yankee Doodle," while the others of the party gloried in the appellations of "Mrs. Langtry," "The Flying Dutchman," "Maccaroni," "Abraham Lincoln," "Blondin," "The Gladiator," and "Just Like Me." The last was a gay little white fellow ridden by our courier.

We returned to the city in fine style, and

my donkey-boy was so ambitious to excel in speed that by vigorous twists, thumps, and punches he hurried his steed into a gallop, and, though sure he was running away, I held on with both hands and enjoyed it until we brought up with a flourish on the pavement in front of the hotel, far ahead of the rest, out of breath, but supremely happy.

The next day we went shopping again, and purchased as souvenirs sandal-wood boxes, scented fans, gayly worked fire-screens, and bottles of scent.

It was in Cairo at Shepheard's Hotel that we made the acquaintance of "Mops," a chubby little English pug-dog, whose chief accomplishment was sitting up on his hind legs and holding a lighted cigar in his mouth. I do not think I ever saw a dog with so much flesh. He was almost as broad as long, and was a source of much amusement to the guests.

Our packing was done with regret, for we were reluctant to leave "Grand Cairo;" but it was necessary to get back to Alexandria in time to catch the steamer for Jaffa.

CHAPTER XII.

STEAMER "RAHAMANIER"—JAFFA—JERUSALEM.

WE all rather dreaded going on the water again; but there was nothing else to be done, so we left Alexandria Wednesday morning for the steamer. The vessel was an Egyptian one, the "Rahamanier," but every thing was clean and comfortable. There were only two first-class passengers besides our party, consequently we had quite a sociable time in the cabin. The ladies were a little seasick, but as the voyage was to be short we made up our minds to endure it patiently "for a season."

Mr. Dattari helped us to pass away much of the time very pleasantly, by telling some of his experiences and adventures while associated with Gordon, up the Soudan. He was an ardent admirer of the brave and gallant officer, and related many incidents connected with him on that memorable expedition.

Most of the time we were in sight of land, and did not suffer in any great degree from that lonely feeling of being "completely at sea."

The first morning we went on deck it was raining, something unusual in that climate. At eleven o'clock Jaffa was sighted, but the anchor was not cast until one.

The ship was riding the waves some distance out from shore, not being able to approach nearer on account of the dangerous rocks in the harbor. It was raining steadily as we descended the steps at the side of the vessel, where, waiting until a wave lifted the row-boat in position, each of us in turn was seized by two Arabs and dropped into it, where we sat serious and silent, holding on with a grip like that of grim death itself.

The small craft was almost upset by every billow that struck it, and some of the ladies were badly frightened, and screamed lustily every time a big wave washed overboard. Strange to say, I was not at all scared, as I thought that was the natural way to land at

Jaffa, and did not realize that this was especially dangerous weather. The little boat carried us as close to the shore as the rocks would allow, and here another mode of transportation was provided—this time on the shoulders of stalwart Arabs. Two of them conveyed Aunt Anna safely over, another shouldered Uncle Robert, and while watching them I was suddenly seized by a big fellow, who walked off through the water with me, evidently minding my weight little more than that of a baby. I had to hold on tight, though, for I did not care to be dropped into the Mediterranean just then. The rest of the party were conveyed in like manner, while the Arabs brought the baggage, and we were all landed safely, with brand-new experiences to laugh at, or shudder over, according to the constitution of the individual, and with the conviction that the *oldest* harbor in the world must certainly be the *worst*.

We walked through more muddy little streets and alleys, saw more dirt, smelled more smells, than ever before in our lives, and finally reached the carriages, wet and bedraggled, but glad to step on something dry and firm once more.

Our hotel was the "Jerusalem," and quite a primitive sort of place it was. On the reading-table was a newspaper of 1870, and some books and periodicals about as ancient. We enjoyed the dinner, though, having fasted since morning, and being thoroughly prepared to appreciate any thing in the shape of food.

We had with us a young Scotchman, Mr. Carmichael, one of Cook's ship-builders. He had been a fellow-passenger on the "Rahamanier," and we learned he was to accompany our party to Jerusalem next morning.

We did not have much chance to explore Jaffa that afternoon, for, besides being very tired, we found a package of mail awaiting us, which was more interesting just then than any thing else could possibly have been.

I am sure you will be sorry to learn that, after all our excitement and fatigue, we got very little sleep that night; I fairly *burn* when

I think of the reason, but as it is an unpleasant subject I leave it to your imagination.

Our uneasy slumbers were broken into next morning at the unearthly hour of three o'clock, as it was necessary to make a very early start in order to reach Jerusalem before late in the night. It was dark, cool, pouring down rain, and dreadfully muddy; so we were glad to find that we were to make the journey in close carriages. Our party numbered nine besides the drivers, and there were three horses to each vehicle. The baggage was to follow on donkeys.

When we had ridden a short distance out of the town, the carriage in front stuck fast in the mud, and the horses either would not or could not pull it out; so we waited there in the dark and rain while the horses were changed and the vehicle hauled out of the mire. The procession started again, and we managed very well until we reached a hill, and then *both* conveyances stuck, and all of us had to get out and walk to the top through the mud. That performance had to be gone through with every time we came to a very steep place during the day. We lunched at a little caravansary on the way, and also rested for awhile at Ramleh, passed through the valley of Sharon, and Ajalon, and saw the house where Tabitha was raised from the dead by Peter.

It was our desire to come in sight of the Holy City before dark, but the hills of Judea were rather too much for us, and it was very late before the end of the journey was reached. The carriages were left outside the Jaffa gate, as no vehicles can enter the city, and we walked through the narrow, rugged streets to the Mediterranean Hotel.

Our baggage had been delayed, and we did not get it until three o'clock. Some of it was quite damp from the rain.

We found among the guests at the hotel our former fellow-travelers, Sir Edward and Lady Lechmere. They expected to take the same tour through the Holy Land that had been planned for us.

The whole of the following morning was de-

JERUSALEM.

voted to much needed rest, as we were by this time somewhat wearied and worn.

Sight-seeing was begun in earnest, however, after lunch. We first visited the Church of the Holy Sepulcher. Here a small taper was handed to each of the party to furnish light through the various dark chapels and passages. The Armenians were holding some kind of service in their special chapel, and we stopped for a few minutes to listen to their weird chanting; then went into the sepulcher itself, the door of which is built very low, so that every one who enters must bend the knee. We put our hands into the crevice of the rock where the cross once rested, and saw the place where our Lord's mother stood weeping for her son.

We then visited Mount Zion and the palace of Caiaphas where Jesus was tried and where Peter denied his Lord.

The guide pointed out the place where King David was buried, and we had a good view of Mount Moriah, Mount Nebo, and the Mount of Olives.

LEPERS OUTSIDE JERUSALEM.

The streets are narrow, crooked, and very dirty—sometimes in steps like a stair-way, crowded with dogs, donkeys, camels, and Arabs. It was hard for us to realize that we were in "the City of David, beautiful for situation."

On our return we passed many lepers, who begged in a heart-rending way for "*backsheesh*, madam, *backsheesh*." They were so repulsive we disliked to get close enough to drop the coppers into their little tin cups. They are not permitted to come inside the city gates, and it was really pathetic to see them crouching along by the road-side in all their poverty and wretchedness.

At the Jerusalem Hotel there was a pleasant party of people from Louisville, Ky. We felt as though they were almost kin to us, coming from so near home.

On Sunday we went to the grand Mosque of Omar, which occupies a part of what was once the area of King Solomon's Temple. The building is very magnificent, with a wealth of rich mosaics, handsome stained glass, and beautiful ornamentations of various kinds. In the center of it is the rock on which Abraham was about to offer up Isaac.

APPROACHING THE MOSQUE OF OMAR.

The Moslems believe that Mohammed ascended to heaven from this rock, and that it tried to follow him, but an angel caught hold of it and held it back. They aver that the rock is now suspended in the air. We certainly did go down under it, but could not accept the tradition concerning it.

We passed along the Via Dolorosa, and saw the Pool of Bethesda, while the Pool of Hezekiah was just back of our hotel.

In the afternoon we rode on donkeys to the top of the Mount of Olives. Aunt Anna went in state, seated in a palanquin—a sort of sedan-chair swung between two mules.

The road up the mount was steep and rocky, but we had a fine view of the city from the minaret on its summit.

We went into the Church of the Ascension, and were shown a foot-print, which the Mohammedans say was made by our Saviour.

Our way then led for some distance through the bed of the brook Kidron, and off on a hill was pointed out the tree on which Judas Iscariot hanged himself.

Passing through St. Stephen's Gate, we visited the Tomb of the Virgin, where small tapers were furnished us again. Inside the sepulcher is a magnificent image of the Virgin richly ornamented with many costly jewels.

We went into the Garden of Gethsemane—a quiet, peaceful place, now in possession of the monks. It is well kept, with walks and beds of bright flowers. There remain some of the same old olive-trees that witnessed the agony of our Saviour on "that doleful night before his death."

The monks presented the ladies with bouquets from the sacred spot, which were pressed and brought home as most valuable souvenirs.

On the Mount of Olives we went down into a kind of subterranean hall, where there were twelve stone niches in the wall. This place was discovered by a duchess, and it was her belief that the apostles used to pray there.

Above ground around the sides of the court were thirty-two stone tablets on which the Lord's Prayer is written in as many different languages.

Returning to the hotel, we passed the Pool of Siloam and the Virgin's Pool; also the place just outside the gate where St. Stephen was stoned.

Our donkeys were not so good as those in

Cairo, but the principal annoyance was the donkey-boys, who got up dissensions among themselves as to whose donkey should have the best place, and all our appeals for "peace" were in vain.

Mr. Gilman, the American Consul to Jerusalem, and his son were stopping at our hotel, and we found them very agreeable gentlemen. They were of considerable assistance to us several times, kindly offering the protection of a guard to attend us through the streets of the city, where it was dangerous for strangers to venture alone.

The tops of the houses were all flat, and easy to walk upon. One night we went up on the roof, and had a splendid view of the Mount of Olives, with the full moon rising over its crest, forming a precious memory for the years to come.

CHAPTER XIII.

JERICHO—DEAD SEA—RIVER JORDAN.

AFTER a pleasant stay of several days in Jerusalem, we prepared to take up our line of march in an easterly direction toward our final destination, and to really "go to Jericho."

I am not an artist, or I would give a sketch of our party as we stood just outside the Jaffa gate, mounted and equipped for the journey. First came the guard, a swarthy Arab of splendid *physique*, dressed in his native picturesque costume and fairly bristling with warlike weapons as he skillfully reined in his fleet charger of the desert; next, Mr. Dattari, who also rode a fiery, mettlesome steed; following him, mounted on horseback, the dragoman, we three girls, Mr. and Mrs. Eastman, and Uncle Robert; after them the cooks and waiters (we had to carry provisions and cooking utensils, there being no hotel at Jericho), who rode or drove cute little donkeys which trotted along complacently beneath their heavy loads of dishes, pans, edibles, etc. Aunt Anna brought up the rear in fine style, seated in a palanquin, and attended by two or three Arabs.

I must not forget to tell something of my horse, which I sincerely hope is the only one of his particular kind in existence. His bones were scantily covered with flesh, and his gait, which was simply excruciating, resembled that of a camel, as he seemed to put forward both feet on one side at the same time.

The road, over the mountains most of the way, was very steep and rugged. In and out we wound among the hills, our procession advancing slowly in single file, the horses carefully placing their feet in the tracks worn by the steeds of former ages, while the sun poured its rays upon us in a perfect deluge of heat.

My noble (?) charger, showing a decided preference for the rear, soon dropped behind; and by no expostulations—beating or thumping, administered by myself and other members of the party—could he be induced to resign his position. I came very near wearing out both my patience and umbrella in ineffectual attempts to make him "get up."

We threaded the narrow pass where the Bible tells us a man once "fell among thieves," but felt safe enough when, looking forward, we saw our dusky guard and his warlike outfit. Lunch was served at the same inn to which the Good Samaritan carried the wounded man, leaving him comforted and cared for. The inn, or khan, is a sorry-looking ruin now, having little to recommend it save sacred association.

When our destination was finally reached, an hour or two before the sun went down, I looked around for Jericho, but failed to see any thing that had even the appearance of the *remains of a city.* Scarcely more was to be seen than the spot where the ancient city stood, and the only buildings within sight were the Greek convent and a little lodging-house, whither we turned our weary horses and sought shelter from the scorching rays of the afternoon sun.

A person not accustomed to riding cannot well endure a whole day's journey on *such a* steed as mine without feeling stiff, to say the least of it. I was more than stiff—hot, sore, sleepy, hungry, and exhausted, both in body and mind. For several days I felt as though I had "been through a grist-mill," and upon lying down seemed as if coming unjointed every time I turned.

A good nap and a savory dinner did much toward restoring failing spirits, and we spent a pleasant evening with traveling acquaintances who had preceded us. The Lechmere party had ridden on donkeys, and were, if possible, more fatigued than we.

It was a beautiful moonlight night, and we enjoyed it wandering about in the grove of lemon, banana, and citron trees surrounding the inn. We ate some sweet lemons, which were rather insipid, being a fruit between the lemon and the orange, and also tried a fresh citron, much better, according to my taste, than the preserved fruit. We gathered the fragrant white star jessamine, and I was appointed a committee of one to pick a banana off one of the trees, which Mary Green tasted to see if it was good. She did not want a second bite, as it was *very green*. Sitting on the little piazza, we sung and chatted until time to retire. After we Americans had sung one of our national hymns the Englishmen present removed their hats and gave us " God Save the Queen." There were not bed-rooms enough to "go round," so a number of the gentlemen had to camp out in sitting and dining rooms.

Next morning an early start was made, and after a ride of several hours over the plains we reached the Dead Sea, and rested for awhile on its quiet shore. I had expected to find this a dreary, desolate place, but it was one of the prettiest sheets of water I had ever seen - clear as crystal, and perfectly calm and smooth. We gathered some beautiful pebbles from the beach, and dipped our hands into and even tasted the water, which was as bitter as quinine.

The gentlemen of the other party, so they afterward told us, went bathing in the sea, and as a result of the buoyancy of the water Sir Edward Lechmere came very near being drowned, but was fortunately pulled out in time by young Mr. Clark, to whom the baronet presented a gold snuff-box as a token of gratitude for his ready assistance. Mr. Gilman joined us just before noon, and he still wore the crust of salt resulting from his briny bath.

Riding to the river Jordan, which flows into the northern extremity of the Dead Sea, lunch was spread beneath the tamarind-trees growing along its banks. We bathed our faces and hands in the sacred stream, cut riding-whips from a thicket near by, and dipped them into the river three times to bring home as mementos, and filled two canteens with the water.

No doubt my old horse could tell something of the fate of my sacred switch, since I wore it into shreds trying to induce him to quicken his steps as we returned to Jerusalem.

The Jordan is a cold, swift, muddy stream, seemingly about sixty or seventy feet wide at

FORD OF THE JORDAN.

the Pilgrim's Bathing-place, from which point we viewed it. We girls sung with great gusto that old revival hymn, "On Jordan's stormy banks I stand," though the banks were any thing else than stormy at that time.

The end of the third day after leaving Jerusalem found us winding our way slowly and wearily back, each one longing as anxiously as did ever Crusader of old for a first glimpse of the walls of the City of David. What a welcome sight it was! and how charming the view as we gazed upon it from the opposite hills and remembered that we were nearing the end of the long day's journey, and had at last really been "to Jericho!" We felt literally the inspiration of the beautiful stanza:

>Jerusalem, my happy home!
> Name ever dear to me!
>When shall my labors have an end,
> In joy, and peace, and thee?

BETHLEHEM.

(138)

CHAPTER XIV.

JERUSALEM—BETHLEHEM—JAFFA.

WE felt sufficiently refreshed next morning to resume our sight-seeing, and decided on Bethlehem as the next place of interest to be visited. This small town is situated on a ridge or hill about six miles from Jerusalem, and contains nearly three thousand inhabitants, all of whom *are Christians*. The drive out was quite pleasant, and among other places passed on the way was Rachel's Tomb, where we gathered handfuls of pretty pink crocuses, that looked fresh and spring-like, peeping up from the stony ground about the old ruin.

From the village itself we had a fine view of the fields of Boaz, where Ruth gleaned in the olden time.

It was with feelings of reverence that we visited the Church of the Nativity, below which were shown the grotto, with a silver star in the floor marking the birthplace of our Saviour, the spot where the infant Jesus lay in the manger, and the tomb and chapel of St. Jerome. It is sad that this place, made sacred to all Christians by its holy associations, should necessarily be guarded by Turkish soldiers in order to keep down dissensions and prevent pilfering and disfiguration by pilgrims of different nationalities and creeds.

The cave or grotto underneath the building is hung with handsome tapestries and gold and silver lamps, while the light above the star is never allowed to go out.

We had lunch at a Latin convent connected with the church, and they gave us to drink some of the native wine, which was rather too sour for our untutored taste.

After buying some exquisite pieces of mother-of-pearl and carved wood-work we entered the vehicles and returned to the city. The carving on sea-shells was prettier in Bethlehem than any we had seen elsewhere.

On the eastern slope of the Mount of Olives,

in the little village of Bethany, we visited what remains of the house of Mary and Martha, saw the tomb of Lazarus, and watered our horses from the stream which flows from the Apostles' Fountain.

One day a shopping expedition was proposed, and a number of us sallied forth in search of something to buy. The principal things were of olive-wood, carved in all imaginable shapes, from a tiny needle-case to imitation books filled with cards of pressed flowers, and collections of fine views of celebrated places around, besides fancy articles of various kinds.

Young Mr. Gilman brought us some "sheikbread," that had been presented to his father, the Consul. It did not look or taste much like bread; was made of flour, honey, currants, and several other things that I could not make out, and dried or cooked in the sun. I should have to be ravenously hungry before I could persuade myself to eat such a doubtful-looking compound.

Uncle Robert had been introduced to Father Stephanos, a Greek monk, and he came to the hotel one morning to show us some of the interesting sights of the wonderful old city. He conducted us first to the Greek Hospital, where we were introduced to the head physician, and invited into his private sitting-room. Soon a servant brought in a large **silver tray**, on which were some goblets of water, two little stands, one filled with spoons, the other empty, and a glass of jelly. It was handed first to Mr. Eastman, but he, not knowing how to proceed, declined to partake. Mrs. Eastman came next, and she asked Father Stephanos what to do. He told her to "take some jelly in one of the spoons, eat it, place the spoon in the empty stand, and drink a glass of water." We all very gravely followed her example, and Mr. Eastman *tried again*. The Arabic coffee was then served in tiny cups, and after a short conversation with the doctor we bowed ourselves out. We were shown through the different wards, and saw where the natives, pilgrims, monks, and nuns were all taken care of, free of charge. Every thing was as clean as could be, and the patients comfortable and well cared for.

Father Stephanos accompanied us to the Church of the Holy Sepulcher, and this time we had a much better view of it than before, from the balcony round the inside of the dome. We also visited a school, where the Arabic children are taught to speak Greek. They sung very sweetly, and allowed us to look over their copy-books. The teacher did not speak English, and all our conversation had to be carried on through an interpreter.

Next the Father went with us to call on the Greek Patriarch, who is one of the four heads of the Greek Church, as the Pope is the one head of the Church of Rome. As he was quite a distinguished somebody, we counted that visit as "a feather in our caps." We were solemnly ushered into a magnificent apartment, and awaited the appearance of the venerable man. After a short time he came in, sweeping along in his rich, heavy robes, and seated himself on a kind of raised platform or throne. We were introduced, and as the Patriarch did not speak our language Father Stephanos had to act as interpreter again. After some conversation refreshments were brought in on a massive silver waiter, the jelly this time being served in exquisite little silver stands, inlaid with gems, while the spoons were of gold, and the goblets of rare and beautiful workmanship. Some small glasses of *"liqueur,"* red and amber, were brought in, which tasted very much like cordial. After drinking coffee from delicate China cups, seemingly as frail as egg-shells, we made our adieus, and walked through a lemon-grove out into the gardens. Here the Patriarch had ordered bouquets prepared for each of the ladies, and we departed with very pleasant impressions of our distinguished host.

We passed on to the Greek convent, and entered the *refectory*, where the boys were at dinner. One of the number was reading aloud to the rest from a large book, which rested on a stand at one end of the room.

JEWS' WAILING-PLACE.

Father Stephanos showed us his own room, and then accompanied us to the nunnery. Here we were conducted into the cell of a nun almost eighty years of age. The room was so small, and the ceiling so low, that it would barely accommodate our party. The old lady sold jewelry which she made of hair. It was a mystery how anybody could live and work in so cramped a place.

After lunch our dragoman took us to the Jews' Wailing-place, where we witnessed the poor creatures' grief, which seemed to be really sincere. They cried and moaned, beating their heads against the rocks in the wall of the temple, and kissing again and again the stones (which have been worn quite smooth in places), some of them reading passages from Lamentations, and others kneeling in silent prayer. It seemed almost sacrilegious to watch them, and after standing for a few moments in silence we quietly withdrew.

We took a walk out to the Tombs of the Kings, and returned through the Russian Consul's grounds, where was pointed out an immense pillar of stone, which is thought to have been intended for use in the building of Solomon's Temple, but was broken in the attempt to excavate it, and has never been removed.

A HOUSE-TOP IN THE EAST.

A very striking feature in the view of the city from the outside was the number of little round domes scattered over the flat roofs of the houses, and we were frequently reminded of what Mark Twain said of Jerusalem: "It was the *knobbiest* city in the world except Constantinople, and looked as if it might have been roofed from center to circumference with inverted saucers."

Before sunrise next morning we were up, bade a long farewell to Jerusalem, and turned our faces toward Jaffa and the sea. We were favored with more pleasant weather on this trip than when on that road before, consequently made the journey in a much shorter time.

Our drive during the morning was uneventful, except that an Arab made an unsuccessful attempt to pick Uncle Robert's pocket. After dinner, however, as we were driving across the plain of Sharon something *did* happen. Aunt Anna and Mrs. Eastman were in a carriage in front of the rest of us, when suddenly Mr. Dattari saw smoke coming from their direction. He immediately jumped down and ran forward to stop the vehicle. When the ladies alighted it was discovered that the cushion on which they had been sitting was on fire. Mrs. Eastman tumbled out in such haste that she bruised her arm a little, and Aunt Anna found a hole burned in her dress, but no serious damage was done. Fortunately, there was a heavy woolen shawl folded on the seat behind, which probably saved them from a serious accident. The only way the flames could be accounted for was that some sparks from the driver's cigarette must have blown in and burned their way through.

We stopped for a moment at Abraham's Fountain, and our courier killed one of the many lizards running about in all directions.

We came in sight of Jaffa before the sun was down, and found there would be plenty of time for a walk before dark. Our guide conducted us to an orange-grove, where the trees were loaded with fruit, and gave us permission to gather and eat as much as we wanted. After having a good deal of fun playing ball with the oranges we bought a large basket of them for about twenty cents, and came away with hands and pockets full.

Next morning we took a walk in the garden of a German baron, where were a great many beautiful flowers; and the rest of the time was spent in writing letters, resting, and lounging.

While standing just outside the hotel making some inquiries of our dragoman, an Egyptian woman, who happened to be a friend of Abrahim's, came by. She stopped to speak to him, and we crowded around to examine her costume, which consisted of a long flowing robe, loose slippers, or sandals, close-fitting head-dress, and a veil of thick black material, which covered half her face below the eyes, and was heavily weighted with rows of coins. She was very good-natured, and seemed to be as much interested in *us* as we were in *her*. Some one asked if she would sell her veil, but she shook her head emphatically, that being probably her most valuable possession.

At half-past twelve every thing was ready, and we climbed into the little boats and were rowed out to the steamer "Ceres," which was anchored just within the harbor.

CHAPTER XV.

STEAMER "CERES"—BEYROOT—SMYRNA.

THERE being just eight in our party, and no other first-class passengers, we had things all our own way on board the "Ceres." Captain Florio and all the officers seemed to consider us as honored guests, and exerted themselves to make our voyage as delightful as possible. It was like a trip on a private yacht, with the weather as calm and beautiful as could be desired. Our state-rooms were on deck, giving us plenty of space and fresh air. Nobody was seasick, nobody was bored, and everybody felt completely at home, while the fare was excellent. We rose at nine or ten o'clock in the morning, were served with a substantial breakfast, and enjoyed greatly the variety of fruits which always accompanied it. I feasted again on fresh dates, and from morning until night we did nothing but have a good time. Every evening after dinner we either gathered on deck and sung and chatted in the moonlight or went down into the saloon and read, wrote, talked, and played games. We found a number of books piled away on a shelf, and brought them out to read. Captain Florio, who had taken quite a fancy to the young people of the party, especially "Mees Suzee," as he called her, hunted up several games for our amusement, and, although he spoke very little English, condescended to play dominos and tripoli with us, evidently enjoying it as much as we did.

There were a great many Turks on board— second and third class passengers—who staid on the lower decks. We felt very sorry for the poor things, especially one night when it rained. They had no state-rooms, and were camping out on the deck, with blankets and mattresses, until they were kindly allowed to come inside the saloon out of the rain.

The captain called our courier "the bad boy," because he was so full of mischief, and seemed to take great delight in teasing him.

One evening at dinner, when Mr. Dattari complained of being cold, the captain rushed off to his state-room and came back with a flaming red blanket, in which he wrapped "the bad boy" head and ears, much to the amusement of the rest of us.

The "Ceres" dropped anchor at Beyroot, on the Syrian coast, early Monday morning, and by ten o'clock we were in the ship's boat rowing ashore for a short visit. How strange and queer every thing looked! How the people stared at us! and how the *beggars did beg!*

We drove out some distance toward the mountains of Lebanon, the highest peaks of which were covered with snow. After a pleasant walk through the garden of Rustum Pasha, ex-governor of Lebanon, we ate ripe bananas off the trees and were allowed to gather all the flowers we wanted.

We stopped for a little while at the Bellvue Hotel, and then went through the silver and silk bazaars.

The ladies of our party were always keen for bargains, and often had amusing experiences. We would enter a little silk-shop and the salesman would hurry to unfold his goods, while Mr. Dattari and the dragoman stood by ready to interpret—Aunt Anna and Mrs. Eastman very much interested, Mary G. a little less so, and Susie and I still less, for we two were never very fond of shopping. Uncle Robert and Mr. Eastman would get chairs and sit down in the street. I would sit for awhile on the low counter listening to the trading, and then go and sit on Uncle Robert's knee and have a laugh at the bargainers.

One day I was occupying my favorite perch, and we two were having a merry conversation all to ourselves, when, happening to look around, I found myself the center of attraction for a crowd of little street Arabs and loafers who had gathered about, and were gazing at me in open-mouthed astonishment, as though looking at a circus. I retired in some confusion, but not before the party had a good laugh at my embarrassment.

In Beyroot we met Dr. Pierce, the gentleman who was so ill on the "Sindh," and were glad to find that he had almost entirely recovered his health and strength, having been for several weeks in the hospital at Jaffa.

One very curious thing I noticed here was the use of prickly-pear plants for hedges. They grow to a height of from seven to ten feet, and have great gnarled trunks and branches like the limbs of a tree. The bloom, or fruit, which is very peculiar-looking, grows out from the edge of the leaves, and in some localities is used for food.

Next day we awoke to find the ship anchored before the town of Larnica, on the island of Cyprus. We went ashore and exhausted the sights in about an hour and a half.

The trip from the steamer to the shore was delightful; the ocean was perfectly calm, and, though I suppose the water must have been a great many feet deep, the bottom could be seen distinctly.

On Thursday we stopped at Rhodes, but as the vessel left before daylight none of us were awake. During the day we cited a number of islands—Patmos, Samos, and others.

Two porpoises made their appearance near the steamer. One of them jumped clear out of the water, so that we had a good look at him.

After dinner one evening Susie and I walked a *mile*—sixty-one times up and down the deck.

Our party composed a "happy family," and we would have been sorry if any other first-class passengers had come on board to break into the little circle.

The next stopping-place was Smyrna, the island of rugs and figs, where the vessel was anchored for several delightful days.

We were rowed in a small boat out to one of the large Italian men-of-war lying in the harbor. The officers received us politely, and as one of them was an acquaintance of our courier he was especially kind in showing us around, even taking us into his own cabin, which was quite a snug and complete little affair. Every thing on board was scrupulously neat, and all seemed to move on like clockwork.

Afterward we went on shore, saw the Smyrna rugs, and invested in figs and candy. The figs were especially nice and unusually low in price, while the rugs were not remarkable either for beauty or cheapness.

Our steamer was quite close to the shore, and the scene on the long street near the wharf was as animated as that on Broadway, New York, with hundreds of queer-looking people going up and down in strangely-fashioned costumes.

We never tired watching them load the vessels. Our ship took on a quantity of cotton and six hundred boxes of lemons, besides many other tropical products.

On Saturday morning the first thing we heard was the firing of one hundred and one salutes from the Italian men-of-war in the harbor, in honor of the birthday of Marguerita, Queen of Italy. We went up on the captain's bridge, and from there had a fine view of the scene. All the great Italian vessels— eleven of them—were beautifully decorated with various colored flags, and a pretty sight they made! That night there was a ball on the largest man-of-war, with three immense electric lights in the bow, which illuminated the whole harbor, lighting the way for the guests. I never saw more brilliant and powerful lights, and cannot describe how bright and beautiful they made every thing.

Numbers of peddlers were constantly coming on board to sell figs. We supplied ourselves abundantly, though already had as many at the table as we could eat.

Sunday was a quiet, uneventful day, the steamer only stopping for a little while at Tenedos. We were anchored a short time at Mitylene, and in the afternoon passed through the Dardanelles and steamed up the Sea of Marmora.

Among the second-class passengers was a beautiful girl, one of the wives, I suppose, of a fierce-looking old Turk. She was anxious to make friends with us; talked a great deal, and seemed puzzled that we could not understand. The Turkish ladies must never let a man see their faces, and when the gentlemen of our party came near this demure maiden always quickly lowered her veil. However, they did get a good view of her face one evening through the window.

Now that this charming voyage was so nearly ended, the weather began to change, and next morning the rain was pouring down in torrents. We managed, however, between showers, to get a view of "Cospoli," as the Turks call Constantinople, and I am sure there never was a finer approach to any place. The city rolls upward in a gentle sweep from the harbor, until the eye, gradually mounting the ascension, rests with delight on the graceful minarets crowning the glorious whole. We could not but hope that the enchantment would not be wholly dissipated by a nearer view.

CHAPTER XVI.

CONSTANTINOPLE—ATHENS.

A LONG, muddy, disagreeable walk through various narrow, dirty streets, with part of the way on an under-ground railroad, brought us at length to the Hotel d'Angleterre, where we found quite a number of letters and papers awaiting us, which we enjoyed to the fullest extent, gathered round a comfortable fire in the reading-room.

Our apartments were beautiful, and quite Oriental in their furnishings—broad, easy, satin-covered divans against the walls, inviting repose, with soft, downy cushions and pillows; pretty little gilt chairs upholstered in blue; handsome mirrors; large easy-chairs, and the curtained recess of the window, made still more inviting by a cushioned seat all round, reached by two or three short steps, making a cozy nook for reading, if we had time for it.

It was raining next day, but our party was not to be daunted by the weather. We donned gossamers and rubbers, and, heavily armed with umbrellas, made our way to Seraglio Point, out on the Golden Horn, where the old wives of the sultan are kept after his Majesty tires of them.

Putting on slippers, we went through the grand Mosque of St. Sophia, taking our first view from the gallery. In this mosque were eight immense columns of porphyry, brought from Baalbec, also some pillars from the Temple of Diana, and the verd-antique was especially handsome. There were several boys sitting around on the floor, and our dragoman told us they were studying for the priesthood.

We went next to the Pigeon Mosque, which was rather a battered-up-looking old building. Each of us threw a cupful of grain into the air, and down came the pigeons, hundreds and hundreds of them, from all directions to feast noisily upon the scattered kernels.

After a visit to the Tomb of Soliman the Magnificent, we went to the mosque which

CONSTANTINOPLE.

bears his name. From the minaret a priest, or muezzin, could be heard calling the faithful to prayers, proclaiming in a loud and monotonous tone: "There is no God but one God, and Mohammed is his prophet! Come to prayers!" Inside the building numbers of people were kneeling on prayer-rugs and bowing their foreheads to the floor, each with his face turned to a niche in the wall in the direction of Mecca.

We walked through the old drug-bazaar, where it seemed to me every kind of herb, powder, and medicine on earth was offered for sale.

Another interesting place was the Cistern of Constantine, with the thousand and one columns. It is a dark, gloomy sort of cavern reached by a flight of much-worn steps, and is now used by the silk-spinners, the dampness being advantageous in the working of that material.

In the silk-bazaars we came across quite a celebrated character (Mark Twain's "Faraway Moses"), a venerable-looking old fellow, who was so sharp at a bargain that we had to guard carefully every particular, and make it a point to pay him about one-fourth the price demanded for an article.

While walking through the bazaars we were accosted on all sides by the shop-men, who would even run out into the street and beg us to stop just for a moment and look at their goods. I never saw a more bewilderingly entertaining place, and could have spent days examining the curious things in the shops — beautiful embroidered scarfs, table-covers, rugs, fine hammered brass, and more curios than I could enumerate.

Among other souvenirs purchased was a tiny sheathed dagger, set with red and blue stones, to be worn as a brooch, the whole thing not more than three and a half inches long.

We also bought some curious bracelets of scented wood, with amber pendants, which were intended simply as playthings, the scent of the wood being greatly strengthened by the warmth of the hands.

One afternoon we boarded a steamer at the

bridge, and took a trip up the Bosphorus as far as the Black Sea. All along the shores were hundreds of summer residences of rich Turks and Christians. The white-marble palace of the late Sultan was pointed out to us, just on the edge of the water, while in the rear, on a rise, could be seen the palace of the present Sultan.

On our return to the hotel one of the first persons we met was Captain Florio, of the "Ceres." We gave him a hearty greeting, but he could not be persuaded to remain and dine with us; consequently we saw but little of him.

The next day being Thanksgiving, we girls concluded to spend it quietly in-doors, especially as the weather was still damp and disagreeable. By this time our wardrobes had become a little the worse for wear, and we bethought ourselves of that famous and necessary "stitch in time."

Friday is the Mohammedan Sabbath, and on that day most of them attend service at some one of the mosques.

We drove out a short distance to see the

Sultan as he went to prayers. The whole city seemed to be moving in that direction, and it was some hours before we caught a glimpse of him. There were thousands and thousands of soldiers in the retinue, many of them Nubians, positively frightful-looking, being as black as soot, and carrying glittering battle-axes. Most of the other troops were in the regular Turkish uniform. His Highness rode in an open victoria drawn by two beautiful horses. He wore a simple suit of black cloth, and was not dressed half as fine as the driver, who sported a magnificent livery of red velvet and gold. The body-guard was mounted on white horses, and kept very close to the carriage of the sultan, who had a rather troubled, uneasy expression on his face. They say that he is afraid to venture outside the palace grounds, and would not go to the mosque on Fridays if the people did not require it.

Constantinople might very appropriately be called "Dog Town," as these animals abound on all the streets, against the walls, and on the pavements, and are so lazy that we had to walk over or around them. They are a miserable-looking set of curs, making night hideous with their howls. However, they are a sanitary blessing to the city, being thorough scavengers, each set having its particular beat, or territory, not allowing any outside dog to leave his own limit, and seeming to know by intuition when their rights are invaded.

That afternoon we bade adieu to Constantinople, and went on board the steamer "Helios," on which we had engaged passage to Athens.

The whole party, except Mr. Eastman, left the table seasick, Uncle Robert excusing himself on the ground that the fish was not cooked exactly to suit him. I cannot be expected to give a very pleasant account of the voyage, which, fortunately, was a short one, the vessel dropping anchor at Piræus, the ancient port of Athens, on Sunday morning.

Open carriages conveyed us over the intervening five miles, and we were all eagerness to get the mail, for we felt sure there must be a quantity awaiting us in Athens. Our courier

THE ACROPOLIS.

had come by rail, so was half an hour ahead of us, and when we reached the hotel met us with a doleful face, and handed out only three letters! How our countenances and spirits dropped as we were conducted, a sad and disappointed company, to our rooms! When these were reached I happened to glance at the table, and there, ranged round the edge, were numbers and numbers of letters—a regular banquet of them. Letters for everybody, with papers in abundance! We then had lunch, and our spirits ascended.

The first thing to be seen in Athens was the Acropolis, so up we climbed and feasted our eyes on the lovely view. The Parthenon is simply fascinating. I caught myself watching it whenever it was in sight while in Athens, and it is a wonder I did not stumble and fall trying to view it over my shoulder from various parts of the city. It is hard to realize the charm that lurks about this old ruin. The open-air Theater of Bacchus on one side of the Acropolis was pointed out, and the guide told us that it once accommodated thirty thousand people. It was here that the "Clouds" was played, which caused the condemnation of Socrates. We also saw a smaller theater, the "Odeum," which was built by a rich Roman in honor of his wife. It was formerly roofed over, but now there are only the ruins of the seats and outer walls.

From the Acropolis we had a magnificent view of Athens and the surrounding country, while in the distance could be seen the place where the battle of Salamis was fought.

Among other ruins on this celebrated eminence are those of a lovely little building called the "Temple of Victory," the image being *without wings*. The reason the Athenians represented the goddess minus wings was that she might not fly away from them.

Just below the Acropolis is Mars' Hill, where St. Paul made his famous address to the "men of Athens." We climbed to the top, and one of our party read aloud the 17th chapter of Acts.

After lunch we drove out to the place where the Pan-Athenian games were celebrated; then saw what is left of the Jupiter Olympus. After visiting the grotto said to have been the prison of Socrates, we stood on the famous rock from which Demosthenes delivered the Philippics.

The Temple of Theseus is the best preserved of all those that are called ruins, and it was there that they showed us the stone tablets with the laws of Solon written on them.

Our hotel was just across the square from the palace of King George of Greece, and every morning about ten o'clock a fine band played under the window of the room in which his Majesty happened to be. We often went up to hear the music, and one morning took a long walk through the palace gardens. The trees were loaded with oranges and mandarins —a kind of fruit something like the orange, but smaller and with a more brittle peel. The grounds were bright with flowers, many of them varieties new and entirely strange to us. It was all so quiet and peaceful, with the wind rustling gently through the trees, that it was difficult to realize we were not far out in the country instead of being in the heart of a great city.

There were numbers of soldiers in Athens, and it was a fine sight to see them promenading up and down the broad, shady walks with their glittering swords and gay uniforms. The Greek costume was very pretty, and reminded me of that worn by the Scotch. The short skirt, instead of being plaid, was white, and made very full, apparently having twenty or thirty yards of goods gathered into it. This was worn over tights, with the feet clad in pointed slippers tipped with pompons. The sleeveless jackets were handsomely embroidered, and on the head were worn red caps with long black tassels hanging from them.

Nearly every thing in the city was made of white marble—the door and window sills and even some of the curb-stones being of this material. It was the most strikingly *white* place I ever saw, and its glitter dazzled our eyes after the dinginess of Constantinople.

Having visited the museums, which were exceedingly attractive, we went to the Hall of Science. This building was also of white marble, heavily decorated within and without with gilding and mosaics, but was so brilliant in the sunshine that we could not look at it longer than a few moments at a time. It was built at the expense of a rich Greek.

We took in the bazaars, where we found many curious things, and went out on the steam-tram to Falero, the summer resort of the Athenians, where we had quite a pleasant time gathering shells and pebbles on the beach, returning after dark to the city.

On Sunday we attended service at a great cathedral. What the priest said was "all Greek" to us, and as there were no seats we had to stand. The singing was very queer, and the service altogether incomprehensible.

In the afternoon we left Athens, not without regret, and boarded the steamer "Venus," which was to carry us to Brindisi.

CHAPTER XVII.

CORFU—BRINDISI—NAPLES—POMPEII

THE weather being too cool to allow much time spent on deck, it was a rather monotonous voyage from Athens to Brindisi. However, we passed the two days pleasantly lounging in the cabin.

I had heard and read all my life of glorious sunsets, but had never imagined that any thing could be half so beautiful as the one we saw on Tuesday evening. We were all down in the saloon reading and talking, when Mr. Dattari called for us to come up on deck. I went immediately, and shall always be glad I did not wait a moment, for the sun went down so quickly we could almost see it drop. The ship was in a kind of strait or pass, with the mountains towering up on all sides. At first the whole scene was flooded with rose-colored light, and away off in the distance could be seen the snow-covered peaks, while the water seemed a liquid, ever-changing rainbow. The sea was calm, and where the prow of our vessel glided through it the shining waves flowed out on either side like the long, graceful folds of a curtain, caught up in the centre, and each fold sparkling and glistening with a different color. As the great, rosy sun dropped lower and lower the mountains changed from deep pink to a dark, rich purple, and their shadows stretched farther and farther out over the water, which continued to reflect all the colors in the sky.

It was a sight to think about, dream of, and remember always, but one not possible to describe in human language. That sunset was worth going to Europe to see, and then and there I felt fully repaid for all the fatigue and discomforts of travel by that one glimpse into what a possible heaven might be.

The "Venus" landed us at Corfu, where we were accompanied by a sanitary officer to another steamer, which was beautifully fitted up, and altogether a charming place for tired and hungry travelers. Mr. Dattari said: "Of course it is nice, for it is an Italian steamer."

After a very refreshing night's rest we were landed safely at Brindisi, where our courier's time expired, but he kindly consented to take charge of us a little farther, so that we might become somewhat accustomed to Italian ways and manners before being thrown entirely on our own resources.

Here it was we began to realize that we had reached the land of music. The first thing we heard at Brindisi was an excellent band, and before we left the hotel three hand-organs played for us under the windows.

We boarded the train and ran along the Adriatic all day as far as Foggia; there changed cars and went straight across the peninsula. As the moon was full, we had a fine view of the Apennines while crossing over them.

Reaching Naples at ten o'clock that night, we drove to the Hotel D'Etrangers, which was delightfully situated on the bay, with Vesuvius smoking away in the distance, and were very much impressed with our first view, by moonlight, of this formidable old mountain.

Next day the weather was so threatening that we postponed our visit to Pompeii, and went instead to the museum, where the things excavated from Pompeii and Herculaneum are exhibited. Some of it was very interesting, and we were highly entertained, but we had seen so many museums (about fifteen, I believe) that we girls were hardly as enthusiastic as we might have been. We were tired of old headless and armless statues, and as for broken pottery, we had seen enough to fill up a small lake! Mary Green said she "had seen *mummies* until she was *mum*," and as for *pictures*, the supply seemed inexhaustible! However, we managed to get a good deal of information as well as fun out of it all, while some of the rest were going into raptures over the old things. We were careful not to miss any thing really important, but museums are all very much alike, and after the great "British Museum" the others seem just a *little tame*.

VIEW OF THE EXHUMED CITY OF POMPEII.

The afternoon was spent in-doors, where we entertained ourselves watching the storm. Such a fury the waves were in as they dashed their snowy spray high into the air, and lashed and beat themselves against the rugged walls of the old Egg Castle, which stood on a point projecting out into the water just within sight of our windows! We congratulated ourselves upon being safe on land just then, instead of at the mercy of that angry sea. The water possessed a strange fascination for me, and I never missed an opportunity of watching the breakers and listening to their weird music.

That night Mr. Dattari left us, as it was necessary for him to go on to Florence. It was a sad leave-taking, for we knew how much we would miss him, as he had been, besides a most efficient courier, a cheery, intelligent traveling companion. We parted with mutual regret, and with the hope of meeting again before our return to America.

Next day the sun shone beautifully, giving us at last an opportunity to visit the ruins of Pompeii. The ride on the cars was pleasant, partly along the sea-shore, with a view of Vesuvius unobscured by the clouds and mist of the preceding day; there he was, in all his glory, calmly puffing out smoke, and looking as quiet and innocent as any ordinary little hill.

On arriving at Pompeii the first thing to be seen was the museum, which contained many curious things dug from the buried city. There were several human bodies, seemingly petrified, with the faces terribly drawn and contorted by the sufferings endured by the poor creatures; also a dog, a chicken, and numbers of skeletons, statues, paintings, household utensils, etc.

The streets of the city were, most of them, about as wide as an ordinary hall-way, and in the flag-stones were still to be seen the ruts worn by cart-wheels more than eighteen hundred years ago. At the corner of each street there was in those days a gong, which the driver sounded as a signal to other drivers to wait until he had driven out, as the streets were not wide enough for two vehicles to pass each other.

We visited the houses of Diomede, Sallust, and the Dancing Faun, besides peeping into various temples, public buildings, chemists' shops, confectioneries, butchers' stalls, bakers' establishments, etc. The mosaics were beautiful. One that especially attracted my attention was the figure of a large dog, lying just inside the front door of one of the houses, and written under it this inscription: "Beware of the dog."

We climbed up into the ruins of the old theater, and, seating ourselves in the "peanut gallery," as Susie called it, had a fine view of the city—a sad but wonderful sight.

On our return we passed the village built on the spot where Herculaneum is buried, but the excavations there do not amount to much.

Sunday was another disagreeable day, but we managed to attend service three times—first at the cathedral, the most brilliantly colored church we had seen, and then at a smaller and less pretentious building.

We stopped for a short while at St. Paul's, just across the square from the palace, the place where the kings of Naples formerly worshiped.

The services were all conducted in Latin and Italian, so we did not feel much benefited, being still *hungry* for a real (English) gospel sermon.

Monday morning we drove around the city, stopping first at a private chapel (St. Severi), where was some fine statuary. Among other pieces was The Veiled Christ, and a veiled figure of Modesty, both of which we admired greatly.

Next we drove to the Monastery of St. Martin, or San Martino, as they call it. This is now used as a museum, and is an interesting place, full of fine Venetian-glass mirrors, candelabra, and table-ware; tortoise-shell cabinets and boxes, queer old china, pictures on silk, and a bewildering variety of beautiful and curious things. The chapel was magnificent. The walls were of the most exquisite mosaics, the floor of marble of different kinds and colors, and the ceiling elaborately frescoed. The altar was of fine marble and precious stones, among which were several pieces of lapis lazuli, and some immense amethysts. On the ceiling of one of the side-chapels was a picture of some one of the saints, which was peculiar in that the feet of the figure were always turned toward the visitor, or seemed to be, in whatever part of the room he might stand. It was a queer effect in perspective. The whole structure was a mass of gold and rare stones, and was the most elaborate thing of the kind we had seen.

In the afternoon we ladies went shopping, and had some funny times trying to make the clerks understand what we wanted. Some of the party talked very loud, as though the people were deaf, and when that failed they took refuge in signs. In the shops were a great many beautiful articles carved out of lava, coral jewelry, shell-work, and many things of tortoise-shell.

A pleasant drive was taken out to the tomb of Virgil, and from there we had a fine view of the far-famed Bay of Naples, the most beautiful, I suppose, in all the world. We were so charmed with its loveliness that we were reluctant to descend the long flight of steps to the city again.

The tomb of Italy's great poet is in a quiet, shady place on the top of a hill, and the grave is marked by a simple slab. We gathered some laurel-leaves from a small tree, and also found some tiny oranges growing near by.

Next day we made an excursion out to Virgil's country, visited Lake Avernus, and went into the Sibyl's Cave, which has been explored to the distance of three miles. We walked in until a little passage was reached, branching off from the main one, when our guide took the lead, Mr. Eastman following another guide, while Mary Green and I brought up the rear, the rest of the party going round another way. After proceeding for a short distance along this passage, which was so narrow there was scarcely room for us to walk, the guide in front motioned for me to get on his back. I looked down and discovered that we had reached water. While I was protesting against this strange mode of locomotion, the light in front disappeared, and we were left in total darkness. Finally, the man picked me up and waded in. I thought Mary Green was being left there entirely alone, and she thought so too, so we both set up a tremendous yell, and I tell you we made those old rocks ring. By this time the water was up to the man's waist, and I was terrified almost beyond expression. After awhile we reached a room called the Sibyl's Chamber, and there, perched on a rock shelf—the water in the room being two or three feet deep—I was delighted to find Mr. Eastman, who had preceded us. Soon Mrs. Eastman came riding in on a *man-steed*, and the guides explained the sights to us. They showed us the orifice in the wall through which the sibyl delivered the oracles written on leaves, as the students of Virgil will remember.

It seems that somebody had come and taken Mary Green back, and Mrs. Eastman concluded to try it in her stead. I do not fancy riding on a man's back, especially when he is wading in water above his knees in the dark.

The explanation of the water in the cave is that the place is below the level of the lake, and when it is full the cave is partially inundated.

We visited Nero's baths, another sort of cave, containing a spring, the water of which was so hot that we cooked an egg in it; then went to Solfatara, a volcano said to be connected with Vesuvius. In one place the smoke was pouring forth, and the steam was hot enough to burn the hand; in others the ground was hot, and sounded hollow when struck.

I picked up some lava that came out of the crater, also some sulphur and arsenic, which was too hot to hold in my naked hand. On the way back we saw some peasant women dance the tarantelle to the music of a tambourine in the Temple of Mercury, where was also a fine echo. We decided not to try to make the ascent of Vesuvius, as the mist and clouds would have obscured the view.

It was a grand sight indeed to watch the old mountain after dark, when he donned his red night-cap of glowing smoke, and calmly stood guard over the beautiful city sleeping far below.

The flowers were abundant in Naples. We saw great baskets of what with us are the rarest hot-house plants sold for ten and twenty cents, and you may be sure we reveled in them all the time we were there.

All pleasant things must have an end, and so we bade farewell to charming.Naples, wondering no longer that the Neapolitans say: "See Naples and die!"

CHAPTER XVIII.

ROME—CHRISTMAS.

A VERY modern-looking railroad train carried us whizzing across the country and landed us finally at a decidedly modern-looking station, in a great, roaring city that they told us was Rome. I must confess to a little disappointment at not catching at least a glimpse of some of the "Roman antiquities" on our first view of this the once "mistress of the world." How could this noisy, bustling place be the "Eternal City," of whose ancient grandeur I had read and studied with such absorbing interest? Who would go to Rome to see glittering shops, street railways, elevators, and other such innovations of these latter times?

We were at the Continental Hotel, and had very nice rooms up on the fifth or sixth floor.

On Sunday morning we engaged cabs and

drove out over a very handsome bridge lined with huge statues across the "Yellow Tiber," past the tomb of Hadrian to the giant of all the churches—"St. Peter's." After listening to some singing in one of the chapels, we wandered about over the superb building, wondering and admiring, for its splendor far surpassed any thing we had seen.

We stood for some time near the bronze statue of St. Peter (which, by the way, is by many thought to be that of Jupiter Olympus, instead of that of the saint), and watched the people as they came to kiss the toe, which is almost worn away by this childish *lip*-devotion. The peasant girls, after wiping off the foot with their handkerchiefs, would press their lips and then their foreheads to it several times. I saw nearly a hundred people go through with this ceremony while standing there. Rough, common-looking men, elegantly-dressed ladies, small boys and girls, while occasionally a little dark-eyed baby would be held up to press its innocent lips to the toe of the statue.

The size of the building grows upon one constantly. To give some faint idea of its immensity, one of the side-chapels (which looks quite small and insignificant, and of which there are a great number), Uncle Robert found by stepping it off to be as large as McKendree Church, in Nashville. The marble-work, paintings, and statues were all so handsome that the other churches we had seen were completely thrown into the shade.

On the way home a man proposed to sell me "the whole of Rome" for only half a franc (photographs, you understand), but I told him I was not in the habit of buying things on Sunday. We would never have imagined it the Sabbath-day, with the shops open, people at work, and every thing going on exactly as on other days.

The stores were nothing like as handsome as those in Naples, and there did not seem to be half so much "Christmas in the air," for it was at this time only a few days until the holidays. In fact, we had all fallen in love with Naples, and it was hard to find another city as beautiful and bright, with its gay shops, exquisite flowers, and crowning glory of the bay.

On our hotel register were the names of a number of barons, lords, and ladies—most of them, I think, belonging to the English aristocracy.

While Mary Green and I were in the reading-room one morning somebody walked in and spoke to us. It proved to be Mr. Carmichael, our young Scotch friend who was with us from Jaffa to Jericho. He had just returned from a trip up the Nile, and was on his way home to Glasgow.

The principal street in Rome was the Corso, about thirty feet wide, with sidewalks (when there were such conveniences) so narrow that two people could not pass comfortably.

Tuesday morning we went to the Vatican, and, as Mark Twain says, "found it truly a wonderful world of curiosities." I cannot tell you half we saw—Apollo Belvidere, Michael Angelo's "Last Judgment," the finest fresco in the world, the "Transfiguration," Raphael's last great picture, the "Laocoon," besides innumerable other beautiful pictures and statues by the world's greatest masters—enough to bewilder any ordinary mortal.

A magnificent gallery was being decorated by the present pope. The ceiling was exquisitely painted, the floor laid in all kinds and colors of lovely marbles, while the walls were an artistic study in themselves. In one place was an immense piece of lapis lazuli, as large as the top of a barrel. Just think of a palace with more than ten thousand rooms! We walked through miles of picture and sculpture galleries, seeing as much of it as we could, and, as our friend Mr. Gorman said, "leaving the rest for posterity." In the *salon*, or hall, were a great many magnificent vases and jars which had been presented to the popes by various monarchs.

We were delighted that evening at receiving the home mail and, besides letters and papers, some pretty Christmas cards and books, showing that, though so far away, we were "yet remembered."

After a visit to the Barbarina Palace, where the principal thing to be seen was the celebrated picture, "Beatrice Cenci," and to the Church of St. John Lateran, we went to see the Santa Scala, a marble stair-way, said to be the identical steps the Saviour ascended at the entrance of Pilate's house in Jerusalem. At all hours of the day numbers of devout Catholics may be seen climbing these stairs on their knees—nobody being allowed to walk up —saying a prayer on each step, then walking down one of the stair-ways placed on each side. The marble steps are covered with wood to keep them from being worn away, and at the top are pictures of our Saviour and the Virgin.

We were much amused at the ignorance as to American manners and customs displayed in conversation by some of the English people we met at the hotel. One lady remarked very seriously that she had a friend whose son had gone over to Virginia, and they were all very uneasy about him. When we inquired the reason, she asked: "Why, don't you suppose the Indians will kill him?" She

THE COLISEUM.

wanted to know "where Virginia was anyhow, and if the people there were *civilized*." She had never heard of the Mammoth Cave, and was evidently quite as ignorant of Niagara Falls.

At the Church of "St. Peter in Chains," was exhibited Michael Angelo's celebrated statue of Moses, and it was indeed a grand conception.

From there we drove out to the Coliseum, that wonderful old amphitheater which once accommodated between eighty and one hundred thousand spectators, and which has since been used for so many purposes—at one time as a stronghold, then as a hospital, after that for a salt depot, a storage place for wool, and lastly as a quarry, for no less than seven large palaces in Rome have been built of stones taken from this marvelous ruin.

After seeing the remains of the baths of Caracalla, which formerly had accommodations for one thousand six hundred bathers, we passed the spot where the "rape of the Sabine women" occurred, and also went through the place where the Circus Maximus stood.

We visited the Roman Forum, saw the Arches of Titus, Septimus Severus, besides the remains of the Temples of Mercury, Saturn, Romulus, and the Vestal Virgins. Driving back through the Corso, we passed the Column of Trajan, where numbers of cats could be seen sleeping in perfect security, basking in the sun; also the Column of Severus, and the fine old fountain of Trevi, which I suppose must be the largest, or one of the largest, in the world.

Friday afternoon at two o'clock we attended vespers in the Church of Santa Maria Maggiore. There was quite a long procession of priests, choir-boys carrying candles, and, greatest of all, the bishop, robed in gorgeous silks heavy with gold embroidery, and his fingers so loaded with jewels that I think he could not have closed his hands.

As the long line filed past us, one of the priests caught the gold lace of his coat on the fastening of Susie's cloak, and the whole procession had to stop for him to release himself, while Susie's face grew redder and redder. It seemed that she was unfortunate where priests and monkeys were concerned.

The music was grand, and, though we could not understand the service, it was solemn and impressive.

Susie and I distinguished ourselves by our purchase of Christmas *goodies*. We bought a lot of small things thinking they were egg kisses, but they turned out to be sandwiches; then our fruit-cake was the most remarkable piece of confectionery imaginable—tasted like tallow, and was so tough that it was impossible to eat it; but the fruit, nuts, and candies were all right, and we enjoyed our feast after all.

On Christmas-eve we gathered around the fire in our sitting-room, and spent the time in conversation, partaking of refreshments—which we girls served in fine style in courses—and singing hymns, closing with "America."

On Christmas morning, after exchanging the merry "Christmas gift," we went through a pouring rain to St. Peter's, where we found services being conducted at nineteen of the twenty-four altars, with singing and prayers going on, and *no one of them* interfering with the *others*. Think what the size of the church must have been! Of course the music was grand, there being two or three large pipe organs. We heard several exquisite, pure, high, soprano voices, which I was with difficulty persuaded to believe belonged to men and boys, there being no women in the choirs.

The priests were on hand again in their magnificent robes, making a gorgeous display.

In the afternoon, while Uncle Robert and Aunt Anna were out, we girls concluded to prepare a surprise for them on their return; so cut "Merry Xmas" out of paper, pinned it on a long red veil, and hung it over the fireplace, arranged our photographs on the wall below, and festooned them with bright ribbons, placed Christmas cards on the mantel, filled in the space with oranges, and illuminated the whole with all our candles, making it look quite gay and festive; then donned our "best bibs and tuckers," and gave them a hearty Christmas greeting as they came in. It was all very enjoyable, and served to remind us of our happy home-gatherings in far-away Tennessee.

On descending to the dining-room, we found it prettily decorated, and an elegant dinner of ten or twelve courses awaiting us. A very attractive dish was a fowl that looked like a pheasant, brought on with the bright plumage still in place. After it had graced the table for awhile it was removed, the feathers taken off, and the delicious meat, juicy and brown, served to the guests. The crowning piece was an immense plum-pudding enveloped in blue blazes, and suggestive of "Merry Old England." Thus we celebrated our first and (I presume) our last Christmas in Rome.

The next day, being Sunday, we started out to walk to the Scotch Presbyterian Church; but, failing to find it, attended service at St. Paul's, an American Episcopal chapel, where Dr. Nevin preached a very fine sermon. The church was festooned with evergreens and flowers, and we greatly enjoyed the services in English and the familiar hymns.

In the afternoon we elbowed our way through immense throngs of people to the Church of St. John Lateran, where we again heard some fine music.

Next day we took a drive outside the city walls, along the Appian Way, stopping at a house which had been excavated near the baths of Caracalla, and at the Columbarium, where the ashes of the pagans were once deposited in urns, and these placed in niches, inside the wall. One of the rooms contained the dust of one thousand people, and looked, as its name implies, like a great pigeon-house. Next we visited the Catacombs of St. Sebastian, and, supplied with little candles, walked through passage after passage lined with cavities containing the bones of seventy-six thousand Christians and martyrs.

On the way back home a horse in one of the vehicles began to kick, and got his leg fastened in the harness, throwing him down. Mary Green and the other ladies in the carriage jumped out, and Miss T., a young girl who had joined our party for the day, was so much frightened that she jumped over two fences and climbed a hill without stopping, and it was some time before she could be induced to return. Finally, they got the horse on his feet again, and we continued on our way, returning by the Via Latina, stopping to examine two tombs which had been excavated, and in which the frescoes and stucco were very well preserved. On the ceiling and walls of one the whole history of the Trojan War was illustrated. In the floor was a deep well, into which the human ashes used to be thrown. We also saw an ancient sarcophagus with some bones in it.

After lunch we visited the Capuchin Monastery, one of the greatest curiosities in all Rome. There were four rooms in a row, opening into each other, and all decorated with the most beautiful and artistic designs in *human bones*— beautiful wreaths, frescoes, hanging baskets made of little finger and toe bones, pyramids and arches of skulls and thigh-bones, while in fancy recesses were numerous grinning skeletons of monks, dressed in their robes and cowls, standing and lying in various positions. If I could only have lost sight of the fact that they were the bones of fellow-creatures, it would have been really beautiful. The monks were once buried in the floors of the rooms, which were filled with earth brought from the Holy Land, and, after their bodies had remained in the ground a certain length of time, were removed to make room for others, and the bones used for decorations. The Government does not allow them to be buried there now, however, and this strange custom has come to an end.

Aunt Anna and Mary Green then went shopping, while Susie and I returned to the hotel, and spent the afternoon very profitably letting out dresses; for traveling had agreed with us so well that nearly all the clothes we brought with us had become distressingly tight.

Our next sight-seeing was a visit to the Capitol, where in one room were the "Marble

Faun," the "Dying Gladiator," and the "Antinoos;" we also went to the Palace Doria, the Farnese Palace, where are Raphael's celebrated frescoes, and attended service on New-year's-day at the Church of the Jesuits, where they sung the "Te Deum" and the "Benedictus." In this church, over one of the altars, is placed the largest piece of lapis lazuli in the world. The whole building was brilliant with more than a thousand candles, and it was filled with an immense crowd of people.

We girls carried some rosaries to St. Peter's Church, and dipped them into the holy water fount, intending them as presents for Catholic friends at home. From the highest gallery inside the cupola we looked down into the church, where the people walking about so far below appeared no larger than *insects*.

We also visited the Quirinal Palace—home of Humbert, King of Italy. The royal stables were magnificent, and we saw quantities of gold and silver mounted harness, splendid carriages, and state turn-outs, besides numbers of fine horses and ponies.

Aunt Anna and I drove out to see an American lady, Mrs. Porter, an aunt of my friend Miss Mamie Black, of Columbia. We found quite a little company assembled in her cozy apartments, chatting and drinking tea. After a pleasant visit we received an urgent invitation to attend an art reception to be given to an American girl, who had made a good reputation as a sculptress, and who was to exhibit on this occasion her latest piece of statuary.

The Church of St. Paul's, outside the city, was one of the handsomest we saw, and as beautiful, in a good many respects, as St. Peter's, with its six columns of alabaster, its superb altar of gold and malachite, and the afternoon sun sending its slanting rays through the richly-colored windows, tinting with purple and crimson its marble pillars and highly-polished mosaic floor.

We carried every thing we had purchased so far to one of the agencies, where they were packed to send to London; then went into several shops and saw them making Roman pearls from alabaster; in another place they were weaving lovely silk scarfs, and we brought away with us souvenirs of each.

After lunch on Tuesday we went to the Church of Aracoeli, the home of the "Bambino." Here are brought people who are maimed or diseased, deluded with the belief that relief is to be had by looking at or touching the little wax image of the Holy Child. A tiny girl recited a long piece in Italian about the "Bambino," which was unintelligible to us.

After visiting the Church of Santa Maria, which is built over the remains of the house where the Apostle Paul lived for two years, we returned to the hotel, packed our valises, and made ready to end our sojourn of several delightful weeks in the Eternal City.

CHAPTER XIX.

FLORENCE.

WE left Rome at twelve o'clock, and arrived in Florence at seven. Next day it rained; consequently we only caught glimpses of *"La Bella Firenze"* through the windows.

We had engaged board this time at a *pension*, or private boarding-house, kept by an American lady, Madam McNamee, whose husband was a sculptor.

The house was originally a palace, and in one of its rooms George Eliot wrote "Romola." Among the guests were Madam Nevada, the sweet songstress of California, and her husband. Several of the other inmates were Americans, and it was quite a comfort to hear English spoken once more.

We girls were amused and rather disgusted one day at twelve o'clock, when a very young red-headed Englishman lounged into the drawing-room on his way to breakfast, and announced with a yawn that he "was up late at a *darnce larst* night."

We visited first the Pitti Palace, the home of King Humbert during his visits to Florence; walked through its galleries of beautiful pictures and statues, saw the splendid mosaics, and were allowed to enter the king's private apartments, which were superbly fitted up with every imaginable luxury and convenience.

The Duomo, or cathedral, is quite a handsome church from the outside, with its immense dome, said to be larger than that of St. Peter's at Rome; but the inside seemed to me rather plain compared to some we had seen elsewhere. However, it was adorned with many fine pictures and statues by the world's greatest masters. The bronze doors of the Baptistery well deserve the compliment paid them by Michael Angelo, who said they were "fit to be the doors of paradise." It is to this Baptistery that the Italian babies are brought when only a few days old to have salt put on their tongues, and their bodies anointed with oil before being dipped into the baptismal font.

Returning to the *pension* one day, we found extensive preparations made for a masked ball to be given to the boarders that night. The stars and stripes were floating bravely beside the Italian colors over the staircase; and the drawing-room was cleared and canvased for dancing. We girls were cordially invited to take part, but, having no desire or inclination to do so, only played the role of spectators.

Madam Nevada, assisted by some of the other boarders, gave a concert for the benefit of the servants, in the saloon on Sunday night. We were disappointed that she selected that time for it, as we would have enjoyed the music, but could not attend any thing of the kind on the Sabbath. Next day, at lunch, in the center of the table was an immense bouquet presented to Madam Nevada by the cook.

For two or three days the rain kept us indoors, until finally we concluded to brave the weather, and made our way to the Uffizi Palace, where were more fine pictures and statues, the principal one being the celebrated Venus de Medici.

The churches of San Marco and Santa Croche—where are the tomb of Michael Angelo and monuments to Dante and Alfieri, and the famous Medici Chapel—were both richly decorated with rare marbles, as were also the churches of S. Lorenzo and S. Maria Nuovo.

The Ponte Vecchio was a queer old bridge over the Arno, lined on each side with small shops, so that it really looked like a continuation of the street. Quantities of the most beautiful jewelry and all sorts of fascinating fancy things were temptingly displayed in these shops, and we ladies found it a charming place for a walk.

The National Museum, which proved to be much more interesting than most museums, and the Palazzo Vecchio, the old palace of the Medici family, were visited, and then we rode for some distance along the Arno to the Cacina. It was a lovely drive, and the view of Florence, nestling at the base of the snow-capped mountains, was one long to be pleasantly remembered.

We enjoyed very much a visit to the studio of Mr. Ball, an American sculptor, who also showed us through his son-in-law's studio, where were some pieces of beautiful statuary, all from original designs. Mr. Ball's "Eve" was exquisite, and he was at work on an immense statue of Barnum, the great circus man.

We walked through the Boboli gardens in the rear of the Pitti Palace; then took another delightful drive up to San Miniato, a picturesque old church on a hill overlooking the city. On the way back we came by the Piazza Michael Angelo, where there is a huge bronze statue of David by that celebrated master.

One night there was considerable excitement in the *pension*, caused by the departure of a young lady and gentleman (who had been boarding there for some time) for Paris, where they were to be married. Quite a shower of rice was sent after them, followed by the customary old shoe "for luck."

It was hard to decide which was the more fascinating—the mosaic shops along the Lungano, or those of statuary on the Via Fossi. They were all very tempting, and I am sure had we been millionaires a great many more of those beautiful things would have found their way across the Atlantic.

One day we witnessed a grand military funeral. The bier, piled high with flowers, was carried on the shoulders of men, attended by hundreds of soldiers and citizens. In the procession were thirty or forty of the Misericordia—a company of persons who unite themselves in a band to perform deeds of charity. They may be seen at all times on the streets of Italian cities, dressed in long brown cloaks, with pointed cowls on their heads, leaving only the eyes exposed, so that no one can recognize them. It is said they are often people of noble birth, who adopt this method of doing good —attending the sick, burying the dead, all unknown to the world, and even to each other.

Mr. Dattari's home was in Florence, and one afternoon we walked across the Ponte Vecchio up the **Via** Bardi to see his residence, which we found to be a large stone house near the banks of the Arno.

In the afternoon we had a delightful ride to Fiesole, a little village on a hill, about three miles from Florence. From this eminence there was a magnificent view of the city, made more charming by a glorious sunset, which verified all we had read of Italian skies and their gorgeous coloring.

After seeing another statue of David at the Belle Arti, and stopping at the Church of the Annunciata, we went to the shops again and selected photographic views of the city, which we found very good, and remarkably cheap.

On Sunday it was trying to snow, but we wrapped up well and went across the river to attend service at a little Scotch Presbyterian Chapel, the nearest thing to a Methodist Church we could find. A young Scotchman (a mere boy) preached, but the sermon was splendid. The whole service was so simple, earnest, and impressive that we gospel-hungry **Americans felt** greatly blessed and benefited.

The Italians are not well prepared for winter weather, and their "scaldini," or little buckets of hot coals, which they carry around on their arms to warm by, do not fill the place of *sure enough* fires. We were thankful for our winter clothes and wraps.

In the English cemetery in Florence are the graves of Elizabeth B. Browning, Walter Savage Landor, Theodore Parker, and the sculptor of the "Greek Slave," Hiram Powers.

We had by this time picked up a number of Italian words and phrases, and we girls had a good deal of fun trying them on people, often with very amusing results. The language is so much like the Latin that even with my limited knowledge of the latter I could understand a great deal that was spoken around me.

The last morning of our stay in Florence I worked up my courage, and went down town a mile or two alone to make some purchases that had been neglected the day before. I did not have any adventures, but must confess to a feeling of relief when I reached the Piazza

Independenza (the square on which our *pension* was situated) in safety on my return.

The time for our sojourn in Florence had expired, and, agreeing that it was next in beauty to Naples, we left at noon for Pisa.

CHAPTER XX.

PISA—GENOA—MILAN.

THE journey to Pisa was a very pleasant one, the beautiful scenery interspersed with an occasional charming marine view. Stopping at a little station on the way, we persuaded an old man standing near to gather us some pretty pink roses that were blooming out there in the January cold. I have some of the dainty beauties pressed and in my flower collection.

After engaging rooms at the "Victoria," our whole party climbed the winding flight of two hundred and ninety-four steps to the top of the wonderful Leaning Tower, and were rewarded by a most beautiful view. It was just at sunset, and the whole landscape — with a distant glimpse of the sea in one direction and the snow-capped mountains in another, and the graceful Arno winding in and out below—was bathed in a soft, rosy light, making a picture

LEANING TOWER AT PISA.

that will remain with us always. The leaning of the tower is more real than imaginary, as we could easily perceive upon looking down from the summit. The most slanting part is toward the base, the top seeming to lean a little the other way, as though trying to hold back. I had never thought of this tower in connection with beauty, but with its graceful, airy look it impressed me as quite a "thing of beauty," especially when its columns and arches were aglow with the pink and purple hues of the setting sun.

We girls raced around the top several times to see how much it slanted, then sat down on the floor and wrote some short letters. I had promised a few lines to a friend from this famous elevation, so hurriedly scratched them off.

The Cathedral in Pisa, that contains Galileo's famous lamp which suggested to him the pendulum, is a superb piece of architecture, as is also the Baptistery close by. In the latter building we heard a fine echo and saw an exquisitely carved pulpit, said to be the handsomest one in the world.

We also visited the old Campo Santo, and spent the remaining time in the marble-shops.

Next our route took us along the shore of the Mediterranean to Genoa, "*la superba,*" through the most picturesque scenery we had seen in Italy. I am sure we must have passed through thirty or forty tunnels, and the glimpses of beautiful landscapes intervening were indeed enchanting. We had quite an amusing time trying to eat our lunch between the frequent plunges into the darkness.

The shops in Genoa were filled with delicate filigree work in gold and silver, which was decidedly tempting, besides quantities of other pretty things. The principal sight was the Campo Santo, or cemetery, certainly the most magnificent we had yet seen. There were great stone galleries hundreds of feet long, with the queerest of tombs and monuments ranged along the walls. The poorer people were buried outside in the central court. One monument had a large figure of Father Time with his scythe, another represented the wife and children of the deceased weeping at the door of his sepulcher, while still another was a death-scene carved in marble, with the family, friends, and physician of the dying man gathered around his bed. Nearly all the tombs were decorated with gaudy wreaths and designs in beads and *immortelles*, while to many of them were attached framed likenesses of the persons buried there.

Of course we visited the Municipal Palace, where they show, besides the relics of Columbus, of which Mark Twain gives such an amusing description, Paganini's violin, which was more interesting to me than any thing else in the collection.

One afternoon we were hunting for the Castle Doria, and happened into an immense university, where we saw some handsome statuary. Finally the Doria Palace was found, and after going through its various apartments and seeing a number of old chairs, frescoes, tapestry, etc., we spent the rest of the afternoon in the shops.

The streets were exceedingly narrow; in fact, some of the houses did not seem to be more than a foot or two apart at the top, as the upper stories projected.

We found snow in Genoa, the first *real* snow we had seen except on the mountain-tops, but it was not very deep.

A most amusing incident occurred one day during a tram-ride through the city. Uncle Robert happened to take a seat in the car by a window-pane that had been broken, and mended with strips of paper. Chancing to touch the glass with his elbow, there was a crash, and the whole thing fell out and was broken into fragments. The driver came running in, and, seeming very much exercised over the accident, began talking to Uncle Robert in a vehement and excited manner. We could not understand what he said, but supposed he must be demanding pay for the loss of his broken glass. The trouble was to find out the amount of the damage. We all tried to comprehend, but it was of no use. Finally the car stopped, and the driver, rushing frantically off somewhere, presently re-appeared accompanied by a policeman, who only added to the confusion and general bewilderment. In the meantime quite a crowd had gathered, and stepping out of the train we found ourselves the center of attraction for an interested group of spectators. Things began to look rather serious, and we were at a loss what to do, when we caught some words which sounded like "*due franc*," so with much relief Uncle Robert handed out two francs and we took ourselves away, glad enough to get out of the scrape with no greater loss. We often speak of it now, and tease Uncle Robert about the time when he came so near being arrested for damaging property.

Mr. and Mrs. Eastman had concluded to leave us for awhile, having decided to take their trip into Switzerland at this time instead of later. They promised to join us again in Venice.

We reached Milan at night, and were delighted with our first view of the city, the streets being brilliantly illuminated with electric lights.

A gentleman at the hotel in Genoa had been very kind about making suggestions as to where we should stop in Milan, and when Uncle Robert exchanged cards with him, lo! he proved to be a *sure enough* count, from Austria.

When I awoke next morning and looked out of the window it seemed that I must still be dreaming, for there, outlined against the blue sky, was a more delicate, fairy-like creation in marble than I had ever imagined could be fashioned by the hands of man.

It was Sunday, also Uncle Robert's birthday, and we celebrated it by attending service at this grand cathedral, the largest and most beautiful Gothic building in the world. After walking around the outside, we went in and heard some splendid music. The ceiling was like cobweb lace—all in pure white marble— and the beautiful stained-glass windows threw their glowing colors over a lovely exhibition far beyond my power to describe. The gorgeous windows represented hundreds of scenes from the Bible, each pane of glass bearing a different picture, and the whole forming what looked to me like an immense jewel in a rich setting.

In the refectory of a convent adjoining the Church of Santa Maria della Grazia is Leonardo da Vinci's celebrated fresco of the "Last Supper" and the "Crucifixion," both rather dilapidated-looking, after more than three centuries of dampness and mutilation. Here also is the Church of Santa Ambrogio, where the kings used to be crowned with the iron crown of the Lombards, and the celebrated "Brera," a palace of "Science and Art."

We girls decided to climb to the *tiptop* of the cathedral. Think of going up five hundred and twelve steps! but we had the best possible view of the building from above, besides getting a bird's-eye view of the city.

While out at the Campo Santo in Milan, we went into the Crematorium, and had the whole process of cremation explained to us. Just before our arrival the bodies of a count and countess had been burned, and they showed us a box of ashes, the remains of a grown person. It took just fifty minutes to cremate a body with gas and two hours with wood. It was not at all a repulsive place; on the contrary, every thing was neat and orderly, and it seemed to me there could not be a better way of disposing of these mortal remains of ours.

After dinner we walked through the long gallery of Victor Emmanuel, a wide, glass-covered passage, lined with beautiful shops and brilliantly lighted with electricity.

After lunch next day we left Milan, carrying away with us—in memory—the cathedral; and I am sure the picture of its ethereal beauty will follow each member of our party through life.

CHAPTER XXI.

VENICE.

WHEN our train sped over the long bridge and into the station at Venice, the "magic city" of our dreams, it was some time after dark.

Instead of climbing into a cab or an omnibus we stepped down into a gondola, and after a long ride through the silent, liquid streets, passed into the Grand Canal and were landed at the door of the Hotel Grand Britannia. Next day, however, we moved to the Victoria Hotel, which we found more comfortable and convenient.

We engaged a gondola for use during our stay in Venice, and after getting a little rested began the pleasant undertaking of seeing the "lions."

After a long ride up the Grand Canal, under the Ponte Rialto and past numerous old

VENICE.

stone palaces, where we saw numbers of "private carriages," as Susie called them, with the gondoliers dressed in uniform, we turned into another canal and visited the Church of the Thari, where are the tombs of Titian and Canova; then on past the Palace of the Doges and the old prison, and under the famous Ponte de Sospiri (Bridge of Sighs).

Our gondolier explained every thing as we went along, but we did not understand very much of what he said.

Next morning we walked down to St. Mark's Square. There are a good many solid streets in Venice, though I do not suppose any of them are more than fifteen feet wide. We entered the Church of St. Mark and feasted our eyes on its lovely mosaics, of which there were forty-five thousand square feet in the ceiling alone. Much of the marble on the inside was brought from Constantinople, and the whole building, with its five domes and gorgeous coloring, reminded me forcibly of an Eastern mosque.

Just above the main entrance are the four

BRIDGE OF SIGHS.

celebrated bronze horses that traveled around so extensively before they were allowed to rest in their present position. Just think of it! These are the only horses that many of the Venetians have ever seen, except, perhaps, one in the zoological collection in the park.

The glass-work and wood-carving were remarkably beautiful here, and we enjoyed very much our visit to the glass-manufactories, where each girl had a bead made with her initials on it.

The Campanile, or bell-tower, was also on St. Mark's Square, and as we were fond (which is the habit of travelers) of going to the top of every thing, we climbed to the top of that, from which point we had a fine view of the city. Opposite the Campanile was a clock tower, and just at twelve the numbers on the face changed, and two life-size bronze figures struck twelve strokes on a bell with hammers which they held in their hands.

In the afternoon we were rowed out to the public garden, where an extensive exhibition building was being erected. This garden is on an island, and here the Venetians come when they want a sight of trees, flowers, and grass.

At the Church of St. George, where we saw a great many of Tintoretta's pictures, Uncle Robert had a funny experience with a fat, jolly priest. The old fellow seemed very friendly and pleasant, and insisted that he "take snuff with him." Being refused several times, he kept offering his little box, until finally Uncle Robert did take a pinch, but, not being accustomed to that kind of refreshment, only held it in his hand. On the way out, however, the box was offered again, and the priest, with many gestures and signs, begged that he take some more. This time my uncle concluded to follow the good father's example, so applied a generous pinch to his nasal protuberance; and then—! while he sneezed we laughed! The jolly priest laughed until his fat cheeks quivered, and we left him standing in the door holding his sides, while the last thing he heard from our party was, "Kchew, kchew, *kchew!*" from Uncle Robert, and a perfect gale of merriment from the rest of us.

In the Church of Santa Maria Salute we admired the fine paintings by Titian—his "St. Mark," and others. Then we rowed again to the Piazza of St. Mark and went into the church for a few minutes to look at the mosaics in the ceiling lighted up by the rays of the setting sun, a brilliant and beautiful spectacle.

In the Doge's Palace is the largest oil painting in the world, Tintoretta's "Glories of Paradise," containing more than a thousand heads and covering one whole end of an immense audience-chamber.

We visited the Venetian lace-school, where the girls were at work on various beautiful patterns.

As it was not possible to enter the Royal Palace on account of its being closed for repairs, we crossed the Bridge of Sighs and went down into the horrible, gloomy dungeons where the poor condemned criminals used to be confined.

We had a pleasant time feeding the pigeons on the square. The birds were so tame they

SCENE IN VENICE.

would light on our heads and arms, and fearlessly eat from our hands the grains of corn which we bought in packages from an old man near by. These pigeons are considered sacred, and no one is allowed to harm them. I brought away a few of their feathers, which I picked up off the ground.

Mr. and Mrs. Eastman arrived next day, and reported a most delightful trip through Switzerland. We were glad to have them with us again.

In the afternoon we took a walk over the Ponte Rialto—which has shops on either side like the Ponte Vecchio in Florence—to the Market, where there were a great many queer specimens of vegetables, flesh, fish, and fowls —but more than all, a remarkable variety of queer smells.

We again entered our gondola, from which the top had been removed so that we could see better, and let our gondolier go where he pleased. He took us through some new streets out to the end of the Grand Canal, within sight of the great railroad bridge.

We girls liked the narrow canals better, for we thought they "looked more like Venice." The Grand Canal resembled too much a river or a wide stream, with its long bridges and small craft. Once in turning a corner into a narrow street our gondola *got stuck*, and we had to back out. That was fine fun, and we enjoyed it immensely. But worse than all was the tiny steamer, that went puffing like a fussy water-bug up and down the main thoroughfare of this romantic city of the sea. It did seem too bad that such a commonplace thing as a steamer should have found its way into Venice.

On Sunday we attended an immense funeral of a countess at St. Mark's. The services were strange and interesting to us. The casket, covered with wreaths of artificial flowers, was placed on a high stand in the center of the church, while all around stood men and boys robed in black, holding lighted candles. The priests, each carrying a candle, marched in and out; sung, chanted, and swung the censers, while the brass band (all the musicians being boys) played a solemn dirge. Then the casket was carried out, preceded by the priests and four female mourners dressed in black, with scarfs on their heads instead of veils. These last each held a silken cord, one end of which was attached to the coffin. The band played a funeral march as the procession passed out of the church and down to the water, followed by an immense throng. The casket was then placed in a large gondola-hearse ornamented with white, silver, and black trimmings, and rowed by four gondoliers in black-and-white uniforms. The mourners entered another gondola, and the whole company glided silently out of our sight.

We had been told that the Cardinal held a confirmation service that afternoon, so went over to the palace and were ushered into a waiting-room. Presently an aged man came in leading a very old gentleman whom we supposed must be the cardinal. He spoke very little English, but we gathered from what he said that he thought we had come to have him confirm a child, and he inquired "whether it was a boy or a girl, and if it was well or indisposed." We finally made him understand that we did not want to have anybody confirmed, and bade him adieu. We afterward discovered that the service we wished to attend had closed before our entrance.

We spent the rest of the afternoon on the square, walking up and down the quay. It seemed that the whole of Venice was out enjoying the beautiful weather. A great many people were sitting at little tables eating and drinking, while the street venders were driving a lively trade—offering every thing imaginable for sale.

We met a very pleasant gentleman at the hotel—young Mr. Carter, from Denver City—and he joined our party next day on an excursion to the school of San Rocco, where was some of the most elaborate wood-carving we had seen; also Titian's "Ecce Homo." There was a library carved in wood that interested me greatly. The books looked so natural that I could not resist the temptation of taking down and examining one of the seemingly well-worn volumes. We went into the Church of the Jesuits, the interior of which was decorated with marble mosaic in imitation of tapestry, curtains, etc., while the floor in front of the altar was made of marble, but looked exactly as though covered with a carpet. Tintoretta's masterpiece, the "Crucifixion," was also in the Church of San Rocco adjoining the school.

We spent a great deal of time in the shops, and you may be sure that when we left our valises were the heavier by a number of lovely little souvenirs in glass, besides a collection of photographs.

The time came to leave this charming place, and one morning we were awakened at the dreamy hour of half-past two, and rowed down the Grand Canal, where every thing was still and dark (the first time we had seen it so). to the railway station. Only one house was illuminated, and there seemed to be a revel of some kind going on there. Carpets were spread down the steps to the water's edge, and strains of music floated out from the open doors and windows, sounding softly sweet and clear to us as we glided silently by in the darkness.

CHAPTER XXII.

VIENNA—PRAGUE.

THE scenery on the journey over the Carnac Alps was grand, especially after dark when the moon had risen; so were the views going through Sömering Pass, until the mists came up and enveloped all in a ghostly garment of white. On one side were great cliffs, hundreds of feet high, with lights from the little villages twinkling among the gorges, while here and there were fairy-like cascades frozen into shining ice, trees laden with hoar frost, appearing as guardian specters, and over all the pure, soft snow glistening in the moonlight. We again passed through a number of tunnels, one of them being over four thousand five hundred feet long.

The train rolled into Vienna about ten o'clock, and then we had a ride that was in decided contrast to our silent departure of the morning from Venice. When we had all climbed inside, and our baggage had been piled on top of an omnibus, the horses started off at a tearing pace over the cobble-stones, while the immense vehicle swayed from side to side, and though we spoke to each other at the tops of our voices, not a word could we hear; could not even hear our own voices, such was the din. I almost held my breath, and am not sure what else I held on to, until we finally brought up with a flourish in front of the Hotel Wandel, when it was indeed a relief to climb out with no bones broken.

The weather in Austria was very cold at this time; but the people seemed to be fully prepared for it, with the houses and furnishings arranged so as to bid defiance to Jack Frost—double doors and windows, tall, white porcelain stoves that reminded me very forcibly of monuments, and in which fires were kept night and day, eider-down pillows and comforts, and beds of down to *cover* with. Mary Green and I used to laugh very much at Susie after she had retired and was all muffled up in the coverings. Nothing could be seen of her but the top of her head, and it looked as though she might be sleeping under a mountain of snow, while her voice sounded as if it came up out of the depths; but it was very comfortable, and we were glad enough ourselves, after a busy day of sight-seeing, to creep into these downy nests.

The morning after our arrival we breakfasted principally on *letters*, as a heavy mail had arrived; then took a tram-ride round the city, which reminded us very much of Paris. The people were extremely kind and accommodating, several gentlemen walking out of their way to show us which train to take, and then instructing the drivers where to put us off.

A very pleasant walk was through the courts of the Imperial Palace to the park, or the "Volksgarten," where was an exact copy of the Temple of Theseus, in Athens, containing Canova's masterpiece, an immense statue of "Theseus and the Minotaur," a superb piece of workmanship, cut out of a single block of marble.

The principal boulevard, "Ringstrasse," was a very handsome street, on which were many of the finest buildings. The imperial stables contained a great many beautiful horses, harness, carriages, etc. The prettiest of all were some black Spanish steeds, sleek and glossy as satin, with tails really dragging the ground; there were also a number of lovely white ones with luxuriant manes and tails.

One of the waiters at the hotel was a curiosity, and became quite a favorite with our party. He was a tiny little fellow, seemingly about ten years of age, dressed in regular evening costume, with swallow-tail coat, long trousers, high collar, white cravat, and always had his hair combed and curled most elaborately. He looked like a second Tom Thumb, but knew how to wait on the table, and required assistance only occasionally in lifting the very heavy dishes. When we entered the dining-room in the morning he was always standing at the door, ready to greet us with a cheery "*Gooten morgen.*"

The chamber-maid, Madeline, amused us

too by coming into our room at night and kissing our hands, for good-night.

We soon learned that it was customary all over the city for the horses hitched to wagons, carriages, and 'busses to go tearing along like mad, while the roar of the vehicles over the cobble-stones was deafening.

We also noticed a great many dogs drawing heavy loads, sometimes being harnessed to a cart piled up with hay, vegetables, or milk-cans, and frequently having as yoke-fellow a man, and occasionally a *woman*.

It was rather an expensive place for shopping, the specialties being amber jewelry, meerschaum pipes, and carved leather-work.

The churches of St. Augustine, St. Peter, and St. Stephen were visited. Workmen were busy on the latter, though it was begun more than six hundred years ago.

On Monday it was snowing, but we did not wish to lose time, so went to the Capuchin Church, in the crypt of which were exhibited copper coffins covered with flowers, containing the remains of the imperial family, Maria

Theresa, her father, mother, and children, Maximilian, and others. In the Augustine Church were silver urns, in which were the hearts of these same royal people.

A delightful drive was the one out to Schonbrunn, the summer palace of Emperor Franz Joseph. Maria Theresa once lived there, and we were shown the rooms at one time occupied by Napoleon. One was fitted up in Chinese style, with all sorts of queer little tables, jugs, screens, vases, unique hangings, mirrors, etc. The covering of a single chair was valued at ten thousand florins, and the decorations of another room at two hundred thousand florins. On the walls of one apartment were paintings executed by the children of Maria Theresa, while still another was adorned with Persian pictures of copper, set in gold and framed in rose-wood. We also saw the apartments of that unfortunate prince, Rudolph, who has recently ended his career so sadly. The grounds were extensive and beautifully laid out, though at this time covered with snow. We climbed to the Gloriata, a kind of colonnade walled in with glass, on top of a hill, and had a fine view of Vienna, and concluded it must be a charming place in summer.

On Tuesday, after waiting quite a long time outside in the cold, we were admitted to the Parliament House, and heard several speeches from members of the House of Commons. It was entertaining, and, though we could not understand what was said, we knew they were discussing the war question.

The "beautiful blue Danube" was certainly the loveliest river we had seen, and with its waters the color of turquois, the purple mountains in the rear, and the blue sky and white clouds above, proved the truth of all that had been told of its beauty.

We spent Wednesday morning at the Palace Belvedere (used as a picture gallery), the building in which the celebrated Congress of Vienna met that banished Napoleon to St. Helena, after the battle of Waterloo. We saw there Rembrandt's finest portrait, a likeness of his mother, which could not be bought for three million florins. The large iron gate at the entrance to the grounds was made by hand, and was very elaborate.

It was a whole afternoon's trip from Vienna to Prague, and not much to be seen along the route, except snow and pine-forests. The hotel proprietor spoke very little English, and the gentlemen had a funny time trying to make arrangements with him about rooms, etc.

Early next morning we went to the Rath House, to see a very curious old clock, which interested us greatly. After a few minutes it began to strike nine. A skeleton pulled the bell-rope and nodded his head at every stroke; a window above opened, and the twelve apostles passed in succession, each stopping for a second or two at the opening; the figure of a rich man shook his head and his money-bags, a vain man looked in a mirror, a wise man held a book, while the cock crowed and clapped his wings. In one of the churches visited was the pulpit from which John Huss preached, and in the Rath House we were shown a fine painting of the great reformer before the Council of Constance.

We also walked through the Students' Gate, on top of which the heads of murdered Protestants were once displayed.

In the old cathedral there was a superb monument to St. John of Nepomuck, made of ten and a half tons of Bohemian silver, exquisitely carved, and, inside of it, a crystal casket containing the bones of the martyr, which are taken out and displayed every fifty years. Our guide told us he had seen them. It is said that this saint was thrown off the Karlsbrucke bridge and drowned, because he would not disclose the confessions of the queen. We crossed the old bridge, and were shown the place from which he was cast down.

After going through the Imperial Palace, in an apartment of which the Thirty Years' War was begun, and where Rudolph lived for two or three years, we went to an old synagogue in the Jews' quarter of the city, the oldest in Europe. Near it was a cemetery, equally ancient, which had not been used for a hundred years. There was not in all Egypt or Palestine any thing as dreary, desolate, and neglected-looking as this old grave-yard, with the broken and dilapidated tomb-stones as close as they could stand, and many of the graves, we were informed, five and six deep.

After seeing the house where John Huss lived, or rather what remains of it, taking a ride all over the city, and looking at its various monuments and public buildings, we returned to our hotel, the Swatzer Ross (black horse), and prepared for our departure in the afternoon.

CHAPTER XXIII.

DRESDEN—LEIPZIG—WITTENBERG.

WE girls often amused ourselves on the long railroad journeys by "telling tales," singing, and playing a game called "Animals," that we had invented for our own pleasure. The trains kept up such a roaring that we could make as much noise as we wished without disturbing anybody, and, being in compartments to ourselves, took advantage of these opportunities to exercise our lungs. Thus we whiled away the hours between Prague and Dresden, reaching the latter place in good time and securing pleasant rooms at the Hotel Weber.

The next day was Sunday, and we started out to find a church somewhere. It was interesting to observe the queer way in which the people attended religious service. They entered the sanctuary with their hands full of bundles, knelt for a prayer or two (turning their heads to see what was going on around them in the meanwhile), arose and walked out, going on with their shopping or work just as on any other day of the week. We saw one young girl at the church repeating prayers with her skates on her arm, and in a few minutes met her on the way to a pond where a large crowd of skaters were having a merry time, with a fine band stationed in a little stand out in the middle of the lake making music for them.

Such bustle and confusion as there was at the dinner-table! We came to the conclusion that the Germans were a very *loud*, jolly sort of people, and the quantity of wine and beer they consumed was alarming.

The Johanneum Museum contained a collection of arms, jewels, and royal robes that belonged to various kings and princes. Many of the swords, suits of armor, and trappings for the horses were richly set with precious stones, making a most gorgeous display.

There was also quite an array of beautiful

Dresden china, besides Chinese, Japanese, Persian, Sevres, etc. Some of the pieces represented horrible dragons, dogs, fish, birds, and all sorts of grotesque figures. Both old and new styles were exhibited, and it was impossible to decide which was the prettier.

After a long drive around the city on Monday afternoon, we wandered down to the lake to watch the skating. Six little boys arranged themselves in a row, with their hands on each other's shoulders. All went splendidly for awhile, until the front one, who was skating backward, tripped over something or somebody, when down they all came in a heap! The people laughed heartily, and the boys jumped up in a hurry to try it over again.

The lake was brilliantly illuminated with electric lights, and, being situated in the midst of a lovely little park, made a delightful place to spend an hour or two on long winter evenings, especially as the music was fine.

Tuesday was devoted to the famous Dresden Art Gallery. It would be folly for me to attempt a description of this splendid collection, and I will simply say that the gem of all was, in my humble judgment, Raphael's "Sistine Madonna." This exquisite piece of work has a room to itself, where the visitor can spend hours looking upon its beauty, which grows more and more attractive the longer one gazes upon it.

On Wednesday we bade farewell to charming Dresden, and reached Leipzig in two hours.

The weather was *very* cold indeed, but inside the house the temperature was so delightful that we felt nothing of the outside discomfort. Early in the morning there was poured into our porcelain stove a lot of what they called "brickets," a kind of composition, something in appearance like peat. Then the double doors were screwed on, and the fire was not disturbed until next morning, the room being kept thoroughly and evenly heated all the time.

The University at Leipzig is situated on the Augustus Platz, a very handsome public square, and an old German porter showed us through one of the buildings. We managed to see most of the city by riding around on the street-cars, but the wind was so icy and every thing so covered with snow that we were glad enough to return to our cozy rooms and beds of down.

Wittenberg, Martin Luther's home, was the next town visited, and our hotel there was the Golden Adler, a house which had been standing four hundred years or more.

At the old Schlosskirche, or town church, was shown where Luther had preached, and the place where he and Melanchthon are buried. The church was being repaired, so of course was very much torn up.

We also visited the old Augustinian Monastery, where Luther had his home, and were shown his study just as he left it, containing many interesting relics of the great reformer --his drinking-cup, wedding-ring, seal, rosary, and some of his handwriting; also portraits of himself and wife, Catherine von Bora, and the *double* chair on which they used to sit.

At Elster Gate was the place where in 1520

he burned the papal bull of excommunication, exclaiming as he did so: "As thou [the Pope], hast troubled the Holy One of the Lord, may the eternal fire trouble and consume thee!"

We went out in the afternoon and bought some very pretty flowers to press and add to our collection; also some photographs of the principal places of interest we had seen in Wittenberg. In one of the shops we had an amusing experience trying to make the man understand that we wanted a picture of Luther's tree. We talked loud and fast, and then we talked slow, and called *tree* by every name we could think of, but the shop-keeper's face still wore a puzzled expression, until at last a bright thought struck one of us and we drew a rough sketch of a tree, with Luther's name written under it. That worked like a charm, and he immediately smiled and handed out some photographs of "der Luter baum," from which we selected the ones liked best, and left with sighs of relief.

Wittenberg was certainly a place of more than ordinary interest, and we remained there until it had all been seen, then made ready to move on to the capital city of the Germans, in which place we had decided to spend several weeks.

CHAPTER XXIV.

BERLIN.

WHEN we arrived at Berlin I felt quite elated on receiving as my share of the mail *nine* of the twenty-three letters awaiting us; and you may be sure no sight-seeing was done until every missive had been read over and over again.

The St. Petersburg Hotel was on that magnificent street, Unter den Linden, which is considered, I believe, the finest in all the world. We had a handsome private parlor, with velvet furnishings, lace curtains, polished floors, and crystal chandeliers, while just before the window was a convenient little desk placed so as to command a good view of the Linden—one of the most charming places for letter-writing imaginable.

From the Royal Bridge to the Brandenburg Gate was about a mile, and we walked the length of it several times, perfectly fascinated by the handsome palaces, university buildings, and splendid shops with which the street was lined.

The Imperial Palace was but a square or two above our lodging, as were also the old palace and the residence of the late Emperor Frederick, then the Crown Prince of Germany.

Every day just at twelve o'clock an immense crowd gathered in front of the old Kaiser's Palace, and as a military brass band passed in front of the building William I. came regularly to his window and stood for a short while saluting the people, being always greeted with shouts and cheers, the multitude seeming wild with delight. We liked very much the old emperor's face, which was kind and pleasant, although it wore an expression of firmness and determination. He celebrated his ninetieth birthday a few weeks after we left Berlin.

Just after we had seen the Kaiser a carriage passed, and all the gentlemen on the street raised their hats to the Crown Princess Victoria, who was seated within. She was a nice-looking lady, quietly and simply dressed, and not at all remarkable in appearance.

Finding after awhile that it would be necessary to spend at least three weeks in Berlin, we concluded to try another *pension*, and so moved to the house of Frau von Schack, a German lady who took only a few boarders. We liked the arrangement exceedingly, as it gave us an opportunity of learning something of German home life. The frau had two grown daughters, and they lived in a flat—the cooking, housekeeping, and every thing being carried on away up on the third floor.

Every evening after the five-o'clock dinner, having spent an hour or two in our rooms, we were summoned to "tea," a dainty meal served in the drawing-room. I did not drink the beverage, but made myself happy with thin sandwiches, little cakes, and lumps of sugar.

It seemed quite novel to sit down to a table in a small dining-room with only nine persons present, and to be waited on by a *girl*. Miss

Smith, a young lady from Detroit, was there studying art. She was very pretty and pleasant, spoke German fluently, and made a charming addition to our circle.

Being again in a land of music, Susie and I found a splendid new piano in our room, and it was an unfailing source of pleasure to us during our leisure moments.

Mr. and Mrs. Eastman were boarding just across the street from us, and near by in a *pension* were two other Nashville friends, Professor and Mrs. Anderson, who were extremely kind in showing us about the city during our stay.

One morning we visited the old and new museums, finding the buildings more interesting than the curiosities they contained. German art was not altogether as fascinating as that of Greece and Italy, though I saw one picture that interested me greatly. It was the original of a little oil-painting that hangs over the mantel in our sitting-room at home—Corregio's painting representing the life-size figure of Io, with the faint outline of Jupiter pressing his lips to hers. The expression of face, the pose of figure, and the exquisite coloring were so charming that it was difficult for me to tear myself away.

Professor Anderson accompanied us to the Philharmonic Concerts, where some of the grandest music in the world could be heard for the trifling sum of fifteen or twenty cents. On the first night the chief attraction was the piano-playing of Miss Haler, a young girl from South Carolina, who made her *debut* as a musician at that time. She was a finished artist, and even those critical Germans seemed to appreciate her performance. Of course the Americans were out in full force, and she was heartily applauded. The orchestra numbered sixty or seventy-five performers, and was simply perfect in time and harmony. The hall was filled with little tables, the audience sitting around drinking beer or coffee, and partaking of light refreshments. A good many ladies present had their hats off, and were busily knitting or crocheting, giving quite a social air to the assembly. Not taking beer, we sat at our table and quietly watched the others until the music began. As soon as the leader of the orchestra raised his *baton* the shades were lowered over the electric lights; there was perfect silence, and as long as the music lasted no other sound was heard in that immense hall. The tables were supplied with felt mats to keep the glasses from rattling, while the waiters tipped about in felt slippers. If any one present had talked or made a disturbance of any kind, he would have been hissed out immediately. I could not but think it a great pity that such rules did not obtain in some of our American audiences. I felt as though roused from a lovely dream when the concert was over, and we were all so delighted that we decided to attend again when an opportunity offered.

In going through the old palace we were required to put on felt slippers, so as not to scratch the polished floors with the soles of our shoes, which proceeding reminded us of our experience in the mosques. This building was very handsome; filled with magnificent furniture, pictures, bric-a-brac, etc. In one of the rooms was an exquisite portrait of the old Kaiser's mother, Queen Louise, who was almost idolized by the Germans for her beauty and goodness.

We attended service on Sunday at the American Church, and were introduced to the minister and his wife, who very kindly invited us to call and see them at their house.

One day we had a new arrival at the *pension* — Dr. Francis, a young physician from Boston. Before he came Uncle Robert had been the only gentleman among eight ladies, and was quite a "lion." The frau was "*awfully nice*" to him; greeted all his anecdotes with the exclamation, "Wonder — wonder — *wonderful!*" while it was most amusing to see her roll up her eyes, clasp her hands, and beg him in the most beseeching way, "*Please* to take another pancake!"

The wax-works were very fine, as were also the National Art Gallery and the grand panorama representing the battle of Sedan.

On Monday we went out three miles through

the Thiergarten, or park, to Charlottenburg, and saw the old palace where Frederick William III. and Queen Louise, the father and mother of the emperor used to live. The palace was handsome, as were also the grounds. We walked over to the mausoleum of these two royal people, and found it beautiful in design and faultless in execution.

Mary Green's birthday occurred while we were in Berlin; and, as the Germans always celebrate these occasions with nice little attentions and remembrances, she was the recipient of some lovely flowers from the frau; also a bouquet from Mrs. Anderson, while we girls made merry over a feast in our own room that night.

The florists' shops were almost irresistible, the windows being piled up with great banks of sweet-smelling blossoms, delicious roses, lilies of the valley, violets, and a thousand other sweets arranged most temptingly.

Aunt Anna, Susie, and I started out one morning to visit the porcelain factory, and managed to find our way, aided by a city map, only taking the wrong street-car once. We found them making all sorts of cups, plates, dishes, etc., and were conducted into one of the ovens where the ware was being *fired* or baked; but it was too warm for comfort, and we did not remain long. One man was molding different kinds of flowers from the soft clay, and using them to decorate the top of a large dish. As I stood looking on he handed me quite a pretty little bunch of roses, which I preserved among my collection of curiosities.

We had an enjoyable time on Frau von Schack's reception night; besides meeting several pleasant German people, Mrs. Anderson came over, bringing with her Mr. Martin, a young American gentleman who was a student in the university.

The Aquarium on the Linden was a most attractive place, containing, besides the fish, many animals, birds, seals, monkeys, beavers, and snakes. It was arranged like a grotto, and I found some difficulty in convincing myself that we were not really wandering about under-ground.

Another interesting place was the Arsenal, where the usual number of small-arms, armor, cannon, and uniforms were displayed.

Mr. and Mrs. Eastman came over after dinner one night to tell us good-by, as they had decided to return home by another route and sooner than we intended to go. It was sad to have our party divided again, but, as it could not be helped, we bade them farewell until we should meet in America.

CHAPTER XXV.

POTSDAM—HAMBURG

POTSDAM is about an hour's ride from Berlin, and I am not surprised that the royal folks of Germany should have selected it as a place of residence, as it is quiet, pleasant, and in every way attractive.

First our guide took us to the old Town Palace, built in the time of the great Elector. When we were there it was occupied in the winter by the young Prince William (the present emperor) and his family, and in the summer they lived in the Marble Palace, also near Potsdam. This old palace was once the home of Frederick the Great, and we were shown his grand apartments, the state dining-hall, reception-rooms, and drawing-rooms, also his own private dining-room, where he ate with his special friends, from a table that could be carried down through the floor and brought up furnished, without the annoyance of servants, who might have listened to the conversation. From the window of one apartment was visible the old lime-tree into which the people used to climb with their petitions to the emperor, the mirrors in the room being so arranged that both sides of the tree could be seen at the same time.

Babelsburg was the summer palace of the old Kaiser, and a more delightful, home-like place it would be hard to find. The grounds were extensive, with charming views of the blue lake through the trees. Hundreds of little boxes were fastened about all through the lawn for the blackbirds, and in the poultry-yard were numbers of chickens, ducks, and other fowls that the Kaiser was fond of feeding from his own hand.

The emperor's rooms were not at all elaborate, but cozy and comfortable, full of little ornaments, treasures, and keepsakes. In one room was a wooden chair that had been made by the Crown Prince, and was highly prized by his father. In his bedroom were photographs of his numerous family, and also a very pretty bust of his mother, Queen Louise.

The guide pointed out to us with a great deal of pride the ivy-covered entrance to the palace, as we came up, remarking: "That same door was used by the emperor himself, visitors, and servants." In the entrance hall a cheerful coal-fire was burning, and on the walls hung a great many antlers of stags shot by the Kaiser, and one large elk's head which had been presented to him by Mr. Vanderbilt.

After we had seen the dining and dancing halls, which were rather plain and unpretending, and the various apartments of the different members of the family, we left Babelsburg and went over to Sans Souci, that superb palace where "Fritz" lived for thirty-nine summers. After enjoying the beautifully laid-out grounds and the view from the terraces in front of the building, we entered the picture-gallery, where was a profusion of works of art collected by Frederick. At the top of the marble steps on one of the terraces were the graves of eleven of his favorite dogs, each one marked by a stone slab inscribed with names, dates, etc. Fritz wished to be buried with his canine friends, and even had his grave dug close to theirs; but his nephew, Frederick William II., would not allow this desire to be carried out. In his apartments, which were most gorgeously fitted up, were many pictures of his favorite dancing ladies, one room being decorated with panel portraits of Madam Barbarina; but when we asked to be shown a likeness of his wife, the guide shook his head, and said: "No, there is none; he did not like her."

In the private dining-room of this palace were various handsome chairs cushioned with satin and down, these being the beds of the dogs, which were fed from Frederick's own fork. In the gallery close by, this eccentric monarch was accustomed to walk up and down, playing on his flute, followed by a number of these same dogs.

Voltaire's room, which he occupied for eight years, was indeed a curiosity, having been fitted up to indulge a queer caprice of the emperor. Voltaire had happened to make some complaint about his apartment on one occasion; so **once,** while he **was** away, Frederick had it fitted up **for him in** a most ridiculous fashion, and it has so remained ever since. Painted on the ceilings, frescoed on the walls, worked into all the furniture coverings, and in every available place, were figures of various kinds of animals and birds, each one in**tended to represent** some real or imagined characteristic **of the unfortunate lodger: monkeys,** because of his resemblance to them; storks, because of **his migratory nature; parrots, because he talked so much; foxes, because he was so sly; peacocks, because of his vanity; a yellow squirrel eating, because he was the color of the squirrel and** because **of his gluttony; and numerous others—all of which naturally enraged and insulted the occupant exceedingly when he returned and saw it. In one of the halls was shown** a hideous portrait **of Voltaire,** representing him **with the face of an ape.** Fritz asked him **to sit for a portrait; Voltaire refused, so** Frederick stationed himself at the key-hole of his guest's room, and painted this caricature in spite of his opposition.

In the Emperor's room was shown a clock that he was in the habit of winding himself, and it is affirmed that just at the moment of his death, twenty minutes past two, this clock stopped, and has never ticked a single time since. In the rear of the palace we noticed a handsome bronze gate, constructed many years ago, which the guide told us was opened only on funeral occasions, and he stated there had been but four of these since it was placed there. It is said that Frederick used to drive out in the afternoon accompanied by a second carriage containing Voltaire and several of his dogs. As the vehicles passed the people would smile and say: "There goes old Fritz, with his favorite dogs and his favorite *monkey*."

The Orangery was another handsome place, so called from the number of orange-trees planted by Frederick. It is now used as a place of entertainment for royalty, the "king's room" being superbly decorated with malachite, presented by Czar Nicholas of Russia. A very beautiful treasure was a table, the top made of amber of different colors, and handsomely set. One of the gardeners gave us some orange-leaves and a tiny specimen of the fruit.

The new palace, the fifth and last we visited that day, was built by Fritz after the Seven Years' War, to show that he was not bankrupted. The most noticeable thing inside was an immense hall decorated with all kinds of shells and precious stones. I have never seen a more beautiful room. The shells were arranged in various exquisite designs, and on the marble columns were bands set with crystal, amethyst, topaz, and other costly stones. In the panels between were imitations of glittering stalactites, and when brilliantly lighted the effect must have been dazzling. One piece of rock-crystal imbedded in the wall weighed sixteen pounds, and in another place was a sea-shell containing a real pearl just as it was formed. In one of Frederick's rooms was a magnificent case or chest for his flutes and music, made of tortoise-shell, mother-of-pearl, and silver, with a small card-table to match. In three of the palaces were spinets on which his music-master used to accompany him, while he played on the flute. All his music-racks were of tortoise-shell and mother-of-pearl.

On the way back we went into the Garrison Church, where part of the eight thousand soldiers living in Potsdam worship. In the pulpit was a sand-glass to time the sermon by (every thing being done with military order and regularity), and when all the sand had run out, which it did in just twenty-five minutes, the minister must say "Amen," whether he had finished his discourse or not. I wonder how some of our home preachers would like that. In this church Frederick the Great was buried in a metal coffin, and the guide gave us some leaves for our floral albums from a wreath that had been placed there by the Crown Princess a short time before.

It was pleasant to get back to Berlin that night and rest, and we spent Sunday quietly in our rooms.

Next day, after bidding our kind friends, the Andersons, good-by, we made preparations for departure, and on Tuesday morning were up before daylight, bade farewell to Frau von Schack and her daughters, and left Berlin from the Frederick Strasse station for Hamburg.

Our hotel in the latter city was down on the Alster, and at night the view out over the water, with the lights glittering on its four sides, was pretty indeed. There were a great many swans gliding over the smooth surface, and the graceful creatures added much to the beauty of the scene.

It was surprising to see the nurse-maids going about with short sleeves, though the weather was cold enough to make heavy wraps and furs comfortable for us. After a long drive through the city, past the harbor, and out into the suburbs, we took a steamer one day, and rode to the end of the Alster. It reminded me of our trip up the Bosphorus, with its residences along the banks. Out in the grounds of many of them were little balconies, built partly over the water, making most delightful retreats, where on hot summer evenings the people sat and drank tea and beer.

The view of the city from that distance was very fine. I had never thought of Hamburg as being any thing but a great business center, and was considerably surprised at its beauty. The people all seemed very fond of flowers, and there were stands and jars of them in nearly every window, even in the houses of the poorest. I was also reminded of Venice by the numerous canals running through the city, and the great number of bridges and boats. Altogether we were much pleased with our visit, and were glad to find that our route would bring us through there again on our return from the north.

CHAPTER XXVI.

COPENHAGEN—HANOVER.

AT Kiel we boarded the steamer "Victoria," which took us across the Baltic to Korsor. Everybody except Uncle Robert was seasick, and, as Tom Sawyer said of his toothache, "it was perfectly awful!" The vessel was so small that it was rocked by every wave that struck it, and we suffered accordingly. It nauseates me even to write about it, consequently I will leave the subject. I was so very glad when land was reached that I felt inclined to get down and hug old mother earth from sheer gratitude.

At Korsor we got something to eat to replace *what we had lost*, and, after crossing the well-cultivated island of Zealand by moonlight, arrived at Copenhagen in time for supper at half-past ten.

The ground was covered with snow, and

next day the sleighs of all shapes and sizes went gliding past our windows from morning until night. Some of them were such cute, trim little turn-outs, with the coachman standing behind driving a double team, and something that looked like a lace counterpane spread from the backs of the horses over the laps of the riders to keep the snow from flying up into their faces.

We found Copenhagen to be a queer old city—especially *old*—most of the buildings seeming to have accumulated two or three coats of the celebrated "dust and mold of ages."

By this time we had dined, supped, breakfasted, and lunched at all hours of the twenty-four. One night we had supper at eleven, and breakfast next morning at ten (How was that for energetic Americans?), though we were often up before daylight, which made things about even after all. I found that I could sleep anywhere, at any time, and under nearly any circumstances, and could eat almost any thing from a fried eel to a Dutch cheese.

Copenhagen's "lions" were ruins of the old Christianborg Palace, which was burned in 1884; the Thorwaldsen Museum, where were displayed many of the beautiful productions of that famous Danish sculptor, and where he himself is buried; the wax-works, and the Danish Folks' Museum. In the latter could be seen several rooms furnished exactly in the style of the north-country peasants of the olden time. Such strange, clumsy-looking furniture, peculiar-looking stoves, funny old beds let into the walls, queer playthings for the children, and rows of plates arranged round just under the ceiling! Last, but not by any means least, Rosenborg Castle, containing a grand display of old-fashioned jewelry glittering with precious stones, badges, coronation and bridal robes of the various kings and queens, besides numbers of rich cabinets, tables, carved furniture, etc. In one of the rooms, opening into the grand Knight's Hall, was a collection of beautiful porcelain, and in another a quantity of exquisite Venetian glass tastefully arranged on gilded brackets. This was a gift from one of the Doges. Still another apartment was called the "Mirror Room," being lined (walls, floor, and ceiling) with glittering mirrors, so that when we stepped inside our images were reflected and re-reflected numbers of times in all directions.

One of the finest groups of figures in the Panopticon, or wax-works exhibition, represented the whole royal family of Denmark, with the Prince and Princess of Wales and the Czar and Czarina of Russia. Another room was lighted by a lamp on a stand, showing the great musician Wagner seated at a piano playing for King Ludwig, of Bavaria, who was standing just outside on a little balcony in the moonlight, which was finely imitated. Still another fine group represented the old Kaiser of Germany, the Crown Prince, Bismarck, and Von Moltke.

It began to snow again very heavily, and we were obliged to give up a trip we had planned into Sweden. All the trains were stopped, and most of the communication from other places cut off. The two or three days we were snowed in were taken advantage of to rest, and I think it was of service to us; at least the home folks some while after received a good many more long letters than they would otherwise have done. I am sure the poor man who roomed next to us must have wished the weather would clear up and let those restless young Americans out, for he heard more singing, laughing, talking, and general romping than might have been expected from the three dignified young ladies who descended to the dining-room and ate their meals so "properly."

The windows of the houses in Copenhagen seemed almost innumerable, the walls being *Argus-eyed* with them from the narrow pavements to the very tops of the queer-pointed roofs, and we concluded the people certainly must be very fond of light and air. In front of many of them were placed small mirrors fastened at such an angle that the occupant of the room could see all that was going on up and down the street. Somebody evidently had curiosity.

We had several pleasant drives about the

city, besides passing the castles and palaces occupied by King Christian IX. and the Crown Prince, the University, and all sorts and kinds of shops and public buildings. In a pretty little park was pointed out a handsome bronze statue of Hans Christian Andersen, that dear old story-teller whose name is precious to all children who love to hear of fairies and fairyland.

The return trip from Korsor had been most heartily dreaded by the ladies of our party, but, as the sea was never calmer or the weather brighter than the day on which we crossed the Baltic for the second time, the fatigue of the long trip was borne cheerfully in gratitude for having escaped the much-dreaded seasickness.

On landing at Kiel, where we had to wait forty-five minutes for the train, our first object was to find a restaurant, as we were ravenously hungry, having eaten nothing since breakfast. When the Germans want refreshment they simply take a glass of beer, and sometimes a piece of bread, and consider it all-sufficient. Accordingly, when we began to

gather up every thing on the lunch-counter—
which was not much after all—the proprietor looked perfectly amazed. We bought his
entire stock of beef, eggs, coffee, and cake,
which we ate, while the waiter looked on in
open-mouthed astonishment. The man made
out an extremely long list of items, and seemed
as serious and concerned over it as though it
had involved millions of money. We then
bought some extra oranges, telling the boy to
put them in a paper for us. He looked utter-
ly bewildered, but finally rushed off, returning
in a few minutes with each orange carefully
wrapped in a *separate* piece of paper. About
that time the train came up, and, gathering
shawl-cases, umbrellas, sachels, cloaks, lunch-
baskets, and *oranges*, we hurried into a carriage, where we were busy putting our things
into the racks when a guard came to the door
and began to gesticulate most violently, repeating over and over again something about
"Herr" (Mr.), pointing to Uncle Robert.
Everybody talked at once, and such a con-
glomeration of jaw-breaking German and Eu-

glish was never heard! Aunt Anna insisted, "I am his frau!" while Uncle Robert assured and re-assured him, "These are my wife and children!" We were finally made to understand that it was a ladies' car, and no gentlemen were admitted. Thinking to find one where all could be together, we again gathered up our belongings and climbed out. Every carriage was full, and by this time quite a crowd of interested spectators had assembled, some occasionally making suggestions. While we stood on the platform in the midst of the hubbub some one advised me to get back into the first carriage, which I did, all the while entreating the others to follow me, as I had no desire to be carried off alone. Uncle Robert gave us our tickets (though he was morally certain "we would lose them before the conductor came around"), and he got into the next coupe. Thus the tumult was quelled, and the train moved off.

After spending another day in Hamburg we passed on to Hanover, and stopped at the Rhine Hotel, where we were again snow-bound for two or three days. We girls manufactured a set of authors with which to amuse ourselves; darned and mended every thing that was out of order, and felt better that our wardrobes were whole once more.

On the third day we determined to venture out in spite of the snow, and as the sun came out in the afternoon we had a delightful ride out to Herrenhausen, the home of the English Georges, passing on the way the Guelph, or *Welfin* Palace, as the Germans have it, where some of Queen Victoria's ancestors lived. In front was a bronze statue of the Saxon horse, represented as rearing and plunging, being wonderfully poised on the two hind feet.

In a museum near Herrenhausen we saw many interesting relics. One room was filled with most horrible instruments of torture— thumb-screws, irons for pinching the flesh, cat-o'-nine-tails, swords for beheading, etc.

The horses in the royal stables were beautiful, half of them pure white, the others cream-colored, delicately and daintily tinted, with tails so long they swept the ground. The royal vehicles were also handsome, especially the coronation carriage of George I., which was gorgeous with gilt and paint, and lined with velvet and satin.

On Sunday we attended a long, tiresome service which, though held in a Lutheran Church, was much more like the Catholic, with altars, candles, choristers, chanting, and so forth.

The Prince of Wales passed through Hanover during our stay there on his way to Berlin to attend the festivities on the occasion of the Kaiser's ninetieth birthday.

A good rest on Sunday afternoon finished up our stay in the city of the Guelphs, and left us fresh and ready for our long journey on the next day.

CHAPTER XXVII.

ROTTERDAM—THE HAGUE—DELFTHAVEN.

TO reach Rotterdam from Hanover took at least twelve hours, but the monotony of the way was broken by several changes of cars.

After our train glided into the Low Dutch country we found there were two things to be seen: windmills slowly waving round and round their great, gaunt arms until it almost made our heads swim to look at them; and the canals, or ditches, cutting into squares and patches the well-kept fields, which looked as though they might have been swept and brushed, so clean and tidy was their appearance. The houses were often of several different colors, with pointed roofs reaching nearly down to the ground on the sides, and sometimes two or three stories up in the gable.

The "Victoria," our hotel, was on the Maas, an arm of the sea, and the Boompjes, or quay, seemed to be the principal attraction of the city. We had a fine position for sight-seeing,

DUTCH WINDMILL.

and it was very pleasant to watch the different vessels as they moved in and out.

Nearly every street ran along the side of a canal, and there were almost as many bridges scattered about as were to be found even in Venice.

The queer head-dresses of the women were objects of curiosity—made of white muslin, flared out around their heads, with great, spiral gold or brass pins sticking over their ears, and often perched on top of all this a ridiculous little bonnet that gave a most comical effect to the costume. Nearly all of the peasants wore clumsy wooden shoes, and had the appearance of walking around with small canoes on their feet. It was amusing to see the little girls jumping the rope, cumbered with this extraordinary foot-gear. What struck me as peculiar was that when these shoes wear out (which they rarely do except by splitting) instead of buying a new pair, that would cost only ten or twelve cents, they get a piece of tin and mend the old ones, and wear them for a long time in that condition.

The markets were well worth visiting, and, though it was drizzling rain, the streets and squares were lined with little stalls, where every thing imaginable was for sale—vegetables, dry goods, hardware, toys, brass ware, china, and all that delights the heart of the ruddy-faced Dutchman, his plump frau, and the rolly-poly children.

In the St. Lawrence Church was a very large organ, and a handsome brass screen. After seeing these we went to the museum and amused ourselves for some time looking at the quaint *Dutch* Madonnas.

There was a canal just under our window, and we were much interested in watching them raise the draw-bridge across it whenever a tall-masted boat came along, which was quite often. The toll was collected in a wooden shoe, fastened on the end of a pole, and handed down from the bank. A great many families live on flat-boats, and we often saw the dogs, cats, babies, and older people comfortably settled at their various occupations on the deck. It is surprising that the little ones do not go overboard oftener; but no doubt most of them learn to swim as soon as they can walk.

On Wednesday we took a guide and made an excursion to the Hague, which is a beautiful little city, much cleaner than Rotterdam, and with its fine parks and drives must be a charming place in summer. Our guide was a droll-looking fellow who kept us constantly amused by his funny English, introducing nearly every sentence with the prefatory expression, "Wall, you thea." In the picture-gallery at the Hague is that magnificent painting, "Paul Potter's Bull," one of the finest *animal* pieces in the world. Our "creamy-eyed" guide, as we had nicknamed him, brought us before this splendid picture, and throwing himself back, while directing our attention to the two principal figures in the piece, remarked with a great deal of pride: "Wall, you thea, now jest look at the *thit down* of dat cow, and *de sthand up* of dat bull." We girls retired behind Aunt Anna, and managed to smother with our handkerchiefs the laugh that would come in spite of our efforts to suppress it.

As it was raining in the afternoon, we took

a close carriage and drove out to the palace of the late queen, first wife of King William III. The building was of brick and not especially handsome on the exterior, but the ball-room was beautifully decorated with paintings by Rubens; and several apartments were fitted up with exquisite embroidered hangings, curtains, wall and furniture coverings, all presented by the Emperor of Japan. We were shown the private sitting-room and boudoir of Queen Sophie, and, as she was a very popular person, they were both filled with handsome presents given her by different friends. It is said that King William, now an old man more than seventy years of age, does not allow his young wife to visit this place, the reason being, our guide told us, "that the remembrance was too great."

The present queen is only twenty-eight years old, and her little girl, the heir to the throne of Holland, has not passed her ninth birthday. The royal family reside in a handsome palace in the city of the Hague.

The weather having cleared off, we had a

pleasant trip back to Rotterdam, and on the way to the hotel walked through an arcade lined with bright, attractive shops, making a beautiful display.

The dogs were worked in Holland just as in Germany, but, instead of hitching them in *front* of the wagons or milk-carts, as they did there, they were *under*, so that sometimes we had to look down among the wheels and axles before finding the dogs. Occasionally there was a man or a woman behind to push, making the work not quite so hard on the poor brutes.

Thursday was a very busy day, and we saw a great deal of Holland. First we went on a steam-tram out to Delfthaven to the old church where John Robertson preached his farewell sermon to the Pilgrim Fathers on the eve of their departure for America. We walked down to the point from which the "Mayflower" sailed, and, looking out over the water, imagined we could see the good ship as she glided off with those brave seekers after religious freedom.

Our next stop was at Schiedam, where we went through a brewery and were shown the process of making "Schiedam schnapps," which, it will perhaps be necessary to explain, is only another name for *gin*. We were all invited to taste it, and I do not think I ever had a more horrible dose, except, perhaps, when I tried some Bavarian beer. It really made me sorry for beer-drinkers. The proprietor showed us one kind of gin that they manufactured for their American trade, and another that they kept for home use. There were three hundred and thirty-five breweries in Schiedam, and they furnish schnapps for the world. Certainly they need temperance-workers there. At Delft, on the way back to Rotterdam, we saw quantities of the quaintest old blue china, such as decorated the cupboards and safes of our great-grandmothers. Some of the ware was purchased to bring home, and then we went down to the canal and returned to Rotterdam by boat. A great many of the canal-boats were drawn by dogs, and I was filled with pity to see the poor creatures pulling away at the ropes, while it was yet more distressing to see a miserable, hard-worked woman tugging with them at the line, and bending her shoulders under the heavy strain.

And the windmills! Mary Green and I counted twenty-nine in sight at one time, some of them grinding grain and others sawing logs.

We were all very tired when the "Victoria" was reached; and, as I was suffering from a raging headache, the girls tried to tease me by insinuating that I had indulged in too much "schnapps." If one sip was followed by such a result, may I never be required to drink a glassful—bitter and foaming!

CHAPTER XXVIII.

AMSTERDAM—HAARLEM—LEYDEN.

AMSTERDAM has been called the "vulgar Venice," and very appropriately too, as it has eighty canals and over three hundred bridges. Our hotel was named the "Old Bible House," because on the spot where it stands was the first printing-office in Holland, where the first Bible in the Dutch language was printed. A copy of this ancient book, kept in the hotel office, is very highly prized and exhibited to all visitors.

Soon after our arrival we went for a walk down through the Jews' quarter, past the dilapidated old house where Rembrandt once lived, and visited one of the diamond *cutteries*, of which there are forty in the city, employing fourteen thousand hands, all of them Jews. The process of cutting and polishing the stones was quite interesting. One of the men told us he had worked twelve hours a day for two years on *one* diamond, which weighed when he began two hundred carats, but of these one hundred and twenty were lost in the finishing. There is a secret in their method of preparing the stones which these Jews refuse to teach to any but their own people, consequently they have a complete monopoly of the trade in that place.

They showed us some fine stones ready polished, and also models of all the celebrated diamonds in the world. The dust is regarded as valuable as the stones themselves, being mixed with oil and used in the polishing.

While down in the Jews' quarter we visited their principal synagogue, which was a rich one, though the building was not particularly handsome.

The Zoological Gardens in Amsterdam rank next to those in London, so of course they were not to be left out in our sight-seeing. We stood for a long while before the lions' cage watching four or five cubs as they romped and played about the old lioness. They were the cutest, jolliest little things imaginable, and looked very much like overgrown kittens as they rolled and tumbled around. The small ponies were lovely, and so was the tiny mite of a white donkey that poked his head out of a stall and begged so piteously for something to eat, and when we went off and left him just cried, kicked, and howled (or rather brayed) like a spoiled baby. We were just in time to see the hippopotamus fed, and truly it was a sight! His mouth seemed large enough to take in a man, and when open was indeed something frightful to behold. They fed him on black bread, which he greatly enjoyed, catching it deftly as it was thrown to him. This one, they told us, weighed five thousand pounds, but they had just lost one which they said was twice as large. In one of the monkey cages was a mother holding in her arms a tiny baby monkey only four or five weeks old. When some bad boys began to tease her with sticks and straws, she hugged the little creature tight with one arm and climbed the **tree with the** other as quickly **as** a squirrel.

The palace was quite attractive, with **its fine** throne-room and great **hall** beautifully **decorated** with carved white marble.

One morning we went through the splendid Ryx Museum, which was new, having been open only a year or two, **and** contained about **two thousand** Dutch **paintings, none of them very remarkable except some** of them *remarkably* **ugly.**

One of the most entertaining of **all our visits was to an orphan asylum, where were** comfortably **housed and fed** about **six** hundred **children.** The poor little waifs seemed **perfectly devoted to the "father," as they called the manager, and he was equally fond of them. They are kept until twenty-one years of age, the boys being taught some trade and the girls learning to sew, cook, and do all kinds of house work.** Every thing about the establishment **was plain and substantial, but** cheerful-looking **and comfortable. In one of** the asylums in **the city both boys** and **girls dressed in uni-**

form, one-half of which was black, the other red. Rather queer taste, I thought, but suppose there was some good reason for it.

We also went into a grand *cafe* said to be the finest in Europe, and certainly its splendor was dazzling.

An earthquake would be very disastrous in Amsterdam, and things would tumble promiscuously; for as you look up and down the street almost every house leans forward because of the settling of the piles, and many seem as if just ready to fall. I could not but rejoice that in our country we have enough room and plenty of good, hard ground upon which to build. Land, with many of these Dutch, is so precious that they run their buildings a great many stories up into the air, while, as I have already said, numbers of people live altogether in their boats on the canals. I never knew before how to be thankful for plenty of *dirt*, and am no longer surprised that these foreigners continue to crowd our American shores, anxious to possess themselves of some of our broad acres of land in the far West.

We found ourselves on Sunday in the city of Haarlem, and went down for service to the Groote Kirche, where we heard the great organ, at one time the largest in the world. It was indeed a powerful instrument, with its five thousand pipes, sixty stops, and three banks of keys. There was an immense audience, and we had the benefit of some fine congregational singing. The church was so large it could not possibly have been heated, so an old woman handed around (that is, if you paid her for it) little perforated boxes with bowls of hot ashes in them, to warm the hands and feet by—something like the Italian scaldini.

In our rooms at the hotel were stoves which burned peat, as they do in Ireland; and we again slept in beds with curtains all around them, making one feel as though creeping into a tent when retiring for the night.

At Leyden, where our party stopped next, was a very large university, and in one of its halls were the portraits of about a hundred and thirty of the professors, all of which interested Uncle Robert very much, but was a "little beyond" the rest of us. We were delighted, however, with the Botanical Gardens, and in the different hot-houses saw some rare and beautiful flowers. The Victoria Regia, that celebrated plant of such immense size, was growing in a pool of water all to itself, and Susie and I were obliged to resist the temptation to pluck and press one of its leaves (three or four feet across) for our albums. On the outside the blue and yellow crocuses, snow-drops, and English daisies, the harbingers of spring, were beginning to show their bright faces among the blades of grass.

We journeyed back to Rotterdam, and, after making another short stay there, traveled on down to Belgium, concluding in our own minds that as regards neatness, frugality, honesty, and general interest we had seen as yet no people who could "beat the Dutch."

CHAPTER XXIX.

ANTWERP—BRUSSELS—COLOGNE.

THOUGH the Grand Hotel in Antwerp was an exceptionally handsome house, splendidly furnished and appointed, it being at the time we were there "out of the season," there were no guests besides our party, and we felt somewhat lonely in the great building; but it was pleasant to be so nicely waited on, as all the servants were at our disposal.

In the Cathedral of Notre Dame were several pictures by Rubens, among them his masterpiece, the "Descent from the Cross," also the "Elevation of the Cross," and various others by his master, pupils, and himself. In his paintings the different faces are portraits of his friends, pupils, servants, two wives, and various relatives. As I walked down the cathedral's broad aisles and drank in the beauty of its glowing windows, exquisite carving, marble columns, and priceless art-gems, I felt as though I had been suddenly wafted back to Italy, the land of gorgeous coloring and rich decorations. The stained glass of one fine window was presented by Leopold II., King of the Belgians, on the occasion of his silver wedding.

In one of the numerous chapels was a head of Christ, painted by Leonardo da Vinci on a piece of white marble. Unfortunately the stone had been cracked across by a fall some time before. A very elaborate pulpit, carved out of oak, was the work of one man who labored at it for *forty-five* years, and then made a present of it to the Church—certainly a royal gift.

After an extensive drive through the city and out to the walls, which were beautifully smooth and green-looking with their covering of turf, we left Antwerp and made our way to Brussels. Every thing there looked decidedly "Frenchy," consequently gay and interesting, with pretty shops, handsome buildings, and splendid boulevards. Thursday was spent

in visiting the queer-looking Hotel de Ville
(or town hall), the palace of the king, also
that of the Count of Flanders, his brother,
whose son will inherit the throne of Belgium,
and the old palace where Maria Theresa once
lived. On the broad steps of the Bourse (or
exchange) were two immense stone lions, one
holding his head up proudly, the other looking sadly at the ground—thus representing
the elevation and depression of financial affairs. None of the pictures in the museum
were particularly noticeable; but the natural
history department was quite extensive and
interesting, being equal to a petrified Zoo,
with almost every known animal displayed;
however, we preferred seeing the living creatures to these "filled up animals," as our
guide called them.

At the Hotel de Saxe, where we were dom-
iciled, they wanted us to pay a franc each because we did not drink wine! Of course inde-
pendent Americans could not stand such
imposition as that, and we moved.

Dismissing the guide one day, we boarded a

street-car and rode clear out to the end of the line, where we alighted and found ourselves completely lost. That part of the city was not particularly inviting, being filled principally with "flying jennies," ragged children, and grocery shops. After wandering about the bewildering streets for a long time, asking questions of the people we met, Uncle Robert came across a man who spoke a little English, and he kindly conducted us part of the way, when we hailed a carriage and were driven to the hotel, as tired a party as ever rested beneath its roof.

In the factories here is made the celebrated Brussels point and Valenciennes lace. A woman in the one which we visited was at work on a piece, one yard of which had required six months' steady labor, and sold for four hundred francs. They showed us a pattern of an exquisite bridal veil made for the king's daughter, who married the Crown Prince of Austria. It employed four hundred persons for three months, and cost thirty-five thousand francs (about $7,000). The Madeleine, the principal shopping thoroughfare, was not as wide as Union Street in Nashville, and just at this time its windows were gorgeous with Easter offerings of various kinds —tremendous red lobsters made of card-board and filled with *bonbons*, all sorts of fish with the same toothsome contents, chocolate eggs full of candy and tied with bright ribbons, some of them large enough to hold a child— all of which were to be exchanged as gifts on Easter morning by the boys and girls. Chocolate, indeed, was a specialty in Brussels, being manufactured in great quantities. Many of the shops sold no other kind of confectionery, but, strange to say, it was very expensive.

The Palace of Justice was a new building, having been completed in 1883. The style was Grecian, and it was wonderfully grand and imposing, being situated at the end of a long street. We had, through our glasses, from the steps of this building, a fine view of the plain on which the battle of Waterloo was fought.

The Parliament House was also new, its

apartments expensively fitted up, and kept in the most perfect order.

The old ducal palace where William the Silent lived was reached after a pleasant walk through the park, and when that had been seen we were tired out and ready for our rooms and rest.

On Palm-Sunday we attended service at the Cathedral. Everybody carried a piece of *green*, and we were assailed all along the way by children selling sprigs of it. On some of these bunches were little images of the "Bambino," gayly dressed in tinsel and gauze, and not particularly remarkable for beauty.

Continuing our journey on Monday, we passed, among other places, Aix-la-Chapelle, Louvain, and Liege, and arrived at Cologne in time for a walk before night. On the square just in front of our hotel was a fine bronze equestrian statue of Frederick William III., and in another platz a splendid statue of Bismarck. The streets were crowded, and it was with great difficulty we made our way along the narrow pavements, which were often not more than a foot and a half wide. I had often read and heard of the *smells* that lurk about this famous city, and must add my testimony to the fact that the various and sundry odors that greeted us were something wonderful for a place with such a name.

The old bridge of boats was a curious structure, made in sections, resting on about forty boats. When a vessel came along two of the divisions were moved out of place, making a gap large enough for it to pass through: we waited to see them clear the way for several, and recrossing the Rhine on the splendid new iron bridge, went to the Cathedral, where a funeral service was being conducted. The building was superb inside and out. The rich stained glass in the south windows was given by the King of Bavaria, and the whole thing was as lovely as a dream. We girls took a guide and climbed to the top of one of the towers, at that time the highest in Europe, then into the room where the five great bells hung. Three of them were ringing at once, and such a deafening noise as they made! It was indeed a real "confusion of tongues," and we could not hear any other sound, even when we screamed at each other in loudest tones. It was a scary sight to look up and see the immense metal monsters swinging back and forth above our heads—the largest seemingly the size of a small house—and was like being up among the thunder-clouds. The view from the tower was grand, with the city lying far below us, and the "castellated Rhine" winding in and out on its way to the sea. It is a large river—would be even in America. We counted the steps ascended, and there were just five hundred and twenty-three. I was glad to have been to the top of one of the highest towers in the world, but I shall not soon forget the weariness that followed the accomplishment of the feat, for when we reached the ground again I was bathed in perspiration, and my limbs trembled so I could scarcely stand.

In the evening we girls varied the monotony of hotel life by accidentally turning over the wardrobe in our room. We were all under it when it fell, but so was the table, which kindly caught the weight, consequently nobody was hurt, and things were soon righted.

Of course we bought some *eau-de-Cologne* at the "original" shop, established in 1695. Over the door was the name of Johann Maria Farina, the inventor of cologne; but then they *all* claim to be his direct successors, so there is no determining the exact odorous descendant. The cologne was very nice indeed, and we carried away as much as it was probable the custom-house officers would allow us, wishing in our hearts that every thing else in this city on the Rhine had as sweet a smell.

CHAPTER XXX.

RIVER RHINE—COBLENTZ—MAYENCE.

WE were now ready for the grand old Rhine, with its castles and ruins, its romantic scenery and historic associations. The steamer "Gutenberg" awaited us at the wharf, and by ten o'clock we were under way, and on the alert to catch the first glimpse of a *sure enough* castle. Just after leaving Bonn our watchfulness was rewarded, for high above on its rugged mountain heights rose Drachenfels ("Dragon's Rock"), or rather what was left of it, while some distance below could be seen another castle, new and complete, with walls, turrets, and battlements in perfect imitation of the old style.

We had lunch on board the steamer, and spent the afternoon on deck, with maps of the river, guide-books, and glasses, looking out the famous places, and greeting with delight each point that came into view as we slowly glided by. That night we landed at Coblentz, and not to get too far away took rooms at the Bellevue Hotel, where our windows opened out on little balconies overlooking the river. Just across the water could be seen the great stronghold or castle of Ehrenbreitstein, called the "Gibraltar of the Rhine," and leading to it a bridge of boats like the one at Cologne, while constantly passing over it were hundreds of German soldiers, whose quarters were at the fortress.

Bright and early next morning our party was ready for a second start, and, after exploring part of the little city in search of something for lunch, boarded the "Elberfeld" and continued the voyage. Now it was that the truly magnificent scenery began to come in view; fine old buildings were passed in rapid succession, situated on top of seemingly inaccessible peaks, some in ruins beautifully draped with mantles of ivy, and others restored, looking stately and stable as they clung to their lofty perches. Our maps gave pictures and names of all the principal towns, villages, and castles, consequently we were prepared and watching for each point of interest before reaching it. I believe the most beautiful of all was Rheinstein, though Rheinfels was the most imposing. Clinging to the tops of opposite mountains, their rough gray walls bearing the marks of time, were New Katzenellenbogen and Thurnberg, or the "Cat" and the "Mouse;" while looking across from opposite rocks stood "The Brothers," Sternberg and Liebenstein; then came Sonneck, Marksburg, Oberwesel, Gutenfels, and many others, all having connected with them romantic legends and historical associations sufficient to fill a volume, if I had time and space to relate them.

You remember the metrical story of Bishop Hatto, who during a time of famine, when his granaries were full of corn, sent out and invited the poor starving people to come and help themselves; then, when they were all inside, set fire to the barn, and while the dreadful holocaust was at its height,

"I' faith 'tis an excellent bonfire!" quoth he;
"And the country is greatly obliged to me
For ridding it in these times forlorn
Of rats that only consume the corn."

. . . .

And he slept that night like an innocent man,
But Bishop Hatto never slept again.

Next morning a messenger came running to tell him that thousands of rats were coming that way. In great terror the wicked bishop fled to his tower on the Rhine, where he shut himself in with strong bolts and bars; but the rats were still coming, and, swimming the river, in spite of the miserable old man's precautions,

In at the windows and in at the door,
And through the walls by thousands they pour,
And down from the ceiling and up through the floor,
From the right and the left, from behind and before,
From within and without, from above and below—
And all at once to the bishop they go.

They have whetted their teeth against the stones,
And now they are picking the bishop's bones;
They gnawed the flesh from every limb,
For they were sent to do judgment on him.

Just about noon our steamer, moving leisurely along, passed this very old tower, and with the greatest interest I watched it until it was out of sight, thinking of the legend of the cruel bishop and his tragical fate. We scarcely took time to eat our meals, but reveled in glorious views all day, stopping for a few minutes in the afternoon at "fair Bingen on the Rhine," a pretty little village nestling close at the foot of a rugged mountain, with a splendid old castle keeping guard high above. On and on we glided up this magic river until all I had ever read or heard of its charm had been verified, and I felt that nothing else in Europe could surpass in grandeur what I had seen that day. The sides of the mountains were in some places almost perpendicular, terraced to the top, and covered with vineyards. It was a puzzle to me how the people managed to stick on the steep sides long enough to cultivate the grapes; and I am sure but for the terraces, the soil would long since have been washed away.

Mayence, where we stopped the second

night, was an exceedingly interesting place, with its Roman towers, barracks, narrow streets, and queer buildings. We were there on Easter Sunday, and went down in the morning to attend service at the cathedral. The music was made by an organ and a brass band, processions were marching around, while priests and chorister boys in red, white, black, purple, and gold, hurried to and fro, swinging incense, chanting prayers and responses, bowing, crossing themselves, bringing in and carrying out silver trays, candles, books, etc., with an amount of ceremony that must have been a great weariness to the people, who took little part in the service except to keep the place in their prayer-books, kneel down and get up at the ringing of a bell, and cross themselves occasionally. Finally the bishop came in and marched up the aisle, preceded by a troop of priests and boys carrying candles, while others followed, two of them holding up the train of his magnificent robe, which was made of heavy purple silk, embroidered with gold. In his hand he carried a long golden scepter, while on the *outside* of his white kid gloves sparkled numerous costly rings. The church was as cold as an ice-house, and I could not but think that constant attendance would be very apt to produce pneumonia and consumption in the worshipers, with no danger of an attack of piety. At night we could see the Rhine from our windows, and the various colored lights on the bridge appeared as strings of sparkling jewels stretched across the water, which shone and glistened like silver in the moon's soft light, while in the morning it was a sight that made our hearts rejoice, to watch the sun rise over the lofty peaks, and brighten up the frowning mountains.

CHAPTER XXXI.

WIESBADEN—FRANKFORT—WORMS.

AN excursion out to Wiesbaden, the most popular of German watering-places, occupied one day very pleasantly during our stay at Mayence, while, with the rich descriptions of things furnished by our fat old guide, and his original rendering of the "Queen's English," we had an amusing trip all through.

Reaching Wiesbaden early, we went out to a little chapel, built as a mausoleum over the remains of his wife by the Duke of Nassau, who owns all that part of the country, and is much beloved for his goodness and generosity. His wife was a Russian princess, who died when only nineteen years of age, and her statue in the mausoleum is an exquisite work of art. The building is Saracenic in style, and is now used for the services of the Greek Church, that having been the young wife's faith.

Around was a lovely park, and on top of the hill a *cafe*, where a fine band played during the season. We girls climbed up to a platform placed in the top of an old tree, and had a magnificent view of a large part of the Rhine country. In the town was a great hall, which was formerly used for gambling purposes, but is now a spacious concert-room. Surrounding it was another beautiful park, and scattered about in all that part of the city were the residences of the nobility.

The place is famous for its hot-water springs, the natural temperature of which reaches 154° F., and a great many people go there for the baths. After drinking of the water and finding it not at all pleasant to the taste, we walked past the Castle, the Cathedral, and through the Colonnade, returning to Mayence that evening much pleased with the day's excursion.

The city of Mayence is in the province of Hesse, and we saw the palace of the Grand Duke of Hesse, who is closely connected with the royal family of England; went to the house where Gutenburg lived, and saw the room in which the first printing-press was set up. On our way to the station, going to Frankfort, the new gymnasium was passed and two old towers, one of which was said to have been, a long time ago, the castle of a robber who went out at night with his men and robbed the *rich* people, giving the stolen goods and money to the *poor*.

An hour's ride brought us to Frankfort-on-the-Main, and, taking a carriage, we drove all over the city, which was indeed a beautiful one. There was a great deal to be seen connected with the Rothschilds—their business houses, winter residences, and summer villas; also the house where Goethe lived, two or three old churches, the palm gardens, and an ancient hall containing portraits of all the German emperors. We were charmed with Frankfort; for there was something about the style of the residences that reminded us of our home cities, and the people were said to be exceptionally refined and intelligent.

One fact impressed us greatly in all these German towns: the large number of soldiers with which they are infested and oppressed. It seemed to me that with such an army Germany ought to be able to conquer *everybody, everywhere.* The people who have to be taxed to meet this enormous expense say it is their ruin, especially now since Bismarck has succeeded in passing the act lengthening the time required for military service.

At two o'clock on Monday we left Mayence by way of the Rhine again, on the steamer "Moltke," but as we had already passed most of the fine river scenery, spent the time in the saloon until landing at the wharf in Worms. What was my surprise to find this last, instead of a city the size of Cologne or Mayence, comparatively a small country town. We had to walk along the road for some distance, there being no carriages or omnibuses at the landing, and a man followed after, hauling our baggage on a little cart. It happened to be Easter Monday, a general holiday with the Germans, and we met a large number of people dressed in their Sunday's best, who stared at us with mouths and eyes wide open as though they thought us to be American Indian savages, and expected us to draw up in line and favor them with a blood-curdling war-whoop! However, we did nothing of the kind, but kept straight on to the hotel, "Old Emperor," which we found nice and comfortable.

While walking along the streets our attention was attracted to a number of strange-looking bunches or bundles of sticks, straw, and mud clinging to many of the chimneys, and were told that these were the nests of storks; that it was considered a piece of very good luck for one of the huge, ungainly birds to build on the roof of the house, the occupant always taking particular care that no harm should come to it.

The chief sight in Worms was the Luther monument, and our guide, for the first time, was a woman. After she had gone with us to all the places of interest—Luther's tree, the old cathedral, monuments, etc.—besides showing us the way to the station and waiting two hours for the train, she refused to take any *pay* for her service! This was the most remarkable incident we had met with in all our travels, and the very surprise of it was almost enough to make us throw up our hats and favor the natives with a genuine war-whoop after all—that is, the younger members of the party. We thanked the lady most heartily, and left the place with pleasant recollections of one person who was willing to do something for the sake of politeness and civility, without the everlasting demand for remuneration.

CHAPTER XXXII.

HEIDELBERG—BADEN-BADEN—STRASBURG.

AT Manheim, on the way to Heidelberg, we crossed a bridge which marks the head of navigation on the Rhine, so that now we had been almost from the mouth to the source of this historic river. Heidelberg is a perfect little gem of a city hidden among the mountains, full of beautiful gardens, fine residences, splendid hotels, and lovely drives.

We found the season much farther advanced there; the trees and plants all budding, and some of the fruit-trees in bloom. During our drive in the afternoon we crossed over the charming river Neckar, which finds its way down from the Alps through the center of the town, lending just enough variety to the view to make it perfect, while high above, overlooking all this, is a fine old castle, or rather the ruins of one, though workmen were busily engaged in restoring it. These ruins are called the "Alhambra of Germany," and are certainly most picturesquely situated.

We drove past a good many of the university buildings and several old churches, the prettiest of which was St. Peter's, all overgrown with ivy.

Every thing in Heidelberg seemed arranged for the comfort of tourists; the grounds surrounding the hotel were beautiful with shady walks, tasteful little summer-houses, numbers of trees, and many flowers. This is a small place, so it did not take long to see the sights, and next morning we were ready to leave.

It required only two hours to reach Baden-Baden, but not so long to decide that it was altogether lovely, situated near the base of the mountains, with the hills around a dark, purplish hue, their sides covered with long stretches of the celebrated Black Forest.

I am not surprised at the story the Germans love to tell of this place. They say that the "angels carried the Garden of Eden to heaven, and on the way dropped part of it, which earthly fragment is now called Baden-Baden!" and in appearance it was indeed a paradise. The grass was so green it reminded us of Ireland, and certainly "nature and art had combined" to create in this spot one of the loveliest places in all the world.

We drove some distance into the Black Forest, which forms a striking background for the town, and all along the way noticed many charming villas most romantically situated. There were quantities of bright wild flowers growing on the edge of the forest, and Susie and I pressed a number of them for our collections.

On the mountain were the remains of an old castle, and close by a new one, or at least one that was new in comparison.

The large hall where the people go for hot mineral water was quite an inviting resort, as was also the Conversation House. In front of the latter the band played in the afternoon, and dozens of chairs and small refreshment-tables were scattered about for the accommodation of guests.

When we awoke next morning at nine o'clock a regular snow-storm was raging, which somewhat changed the aspect of affairs, though Baden was still charming, even under these chilling circumstances.

When we reached Strasburg at lunch-time it was raining, but this did not prevent our going over to the Cathedral, as that was what we had come to see. The quantity of stained glass in this building was immense; the windows on one side were five hundred years old, and the rose window in the end, called the Marigold, was truly a gem. Most of the old glass was saved from destruction during the siege of 1871, by being taken out and placed down in the crypt. We did not go up into the tower, as there was a mist which would have obscured the view, besides we had already satisfied our ambition for climbing by ascending the one at Cologne, and were not ready to try another so soon. There was a beautiful piece of work in the church, consisting of a sculptured pillar, executed by the daughter of the architect of the building. The most wonderful thing was the clock, in the north transept of the Cathedral. This has been so often and so minutely described that it seems almost presumptuous in me to attempt any thing further, therefore I will only tell what I saw as we watched it for an hour. It struck every fifteen minutes, and the marvelous figures with which it was adorned did marvelous things. There were two galleries, on one of which was a skeleton which struck the hours on a bell which he held in his hand. The first quarter-hour was sounded alternately by an angel and a child, the second by a youth, the third by a middle-aged man, and the fourth by an old man. Every hour a tiny cherub turned over a sand-glass and one of the twelve apostles moved forward in front of the figure of the Saviour. Each day of the week was represented by a chariot, which moved forward in its niche; and over all was the cock, which flapped its wings and crowed. The astronomical part of the clock, showing all the different changes of the moon, positions of the planets, etc., is to be wound up every *nine hundred* and *ninety-nine years,* while the *time* part is wound once a week.

We staid for some time listening to the vespers, and then walked through the old arcades, where a great variety of articles were displayed for sale.

The women in this place wore strange head-dresses, consisting of immense ribbon bows of various colors pinned on top of their heads, flaring out in the breeze, and looking exactly like sails. We were told that the Protestants dressed in green, and the Catholics in red.

The university buildings were quite extensive, and altogether as fine as any we had seen, or finer.

The houses had curious pointed roofs—the roofs themselves containing a number of stories. Many of them looked so ancient that we wondered if it was not dangerous to step inside.

Having seen the principal sights of Strasburg—the Cathedral and its wonderful clock—we next day started for Switzerland, prepared for snow, ice, glaciers, bowlders, lakes, and mountains.

CHAPTER XXXIII.

BASLE—LUCERNE—BERNE.

BASLE, our next stopping-place, is one of the largest cities in Switzerland, though Geneva and a few others are better known.

The old cathedral, a Protestant church, contains the tomb of Erasmus. It has a fine organ and some rare stained glass windows. From a terrace in the rear we had a splendid view of the city, the Upper Rhine, and the highest part of the Black Forest.

The town is divided into two parts, great and little Basle, and at each end of the bridge, which commands fine views up and down the river, are several bronze dragons.

We only tarried long enough in Basle to see the sights and rest a short while, then continued our journey to Lucerne, through part of the Black Forest, skirting around Mt. Jura, and finally plunging into a long tunnel which runs through the mountain. The scenery was grand, though often obscured by snow, which takes the place of rain in the April showers among the Alps. We saw many beautifully cultivated valleys, high and rugged mountains, with here and there cozy little chalets dotted between, having long sloping roofs, carved gables, and eaves projecting so far as almost to touch the ground, and in many instances serving instead of porches.

We lodged at the hotel St. Gotthard close to Lake Lucerne, and the first thing I saw on opening my eyes in the morning and glancing out of the window was the sunlight flooding the tops of the snow-covered peaks.

After breakfast we walked down to the lake and feasted our eyes on its loveliness. O the beauty of it! As blue as the Danube, set off by a background of great mountains covered with robes of shining snow, their heads out of sight in the clouds; and later on the sunset, first tinging the white mantles of the stately old monarchs with a soft and delicate pink, then changing their hue in a few moments to regal purple and gold, as though arraying them for some fabled banquet of the mountain gods. Across part of the lake was an old bridge—a rickety, wooden affair, having all along its top three-cornered oil-paintings, which seemed to be very ancient, and must, I am sure, have had an interesting history connected with them. All about the place we noticed quantities of exquisite wood-carving—every thing imaginable that could be fashioned in wood, from a bear to a box of jack-straws. The most beautiful piece was the celebrated Lion of Lucerne, carved out of the face of a solid cliff from Thorwaldsen's finest design. Of all the sculpture we had seen, this figure was the gem, and we stood for a long time gazing upon it, fascinated by its expression of majesty and power.

After lunch on Monday a trip was taken on the small steamer "Helvetia" up the lake as far as Weggis, a pretty little place at the foot of the Righi. It is here that tourists generally begin the ascent of the mountain, but as it was too cold for us to attempt it we wandered around below, gathered handfuls of wild flowers, and enjoyed the matchless scenery.

On our return to Lucerne a walk was proposed to the old wall or fortifications, after which Mary Green and I went through what is called the Glacier Garden, where we saw holes worn in the rocks by the passage of a glacier, with numerous bowlders and debris scattered along its track.

On the shores of the lake were lovely chateaux, picturesque little boat-houses, and handsome residences with green and velvety lawns sloping down to the water. It was just as though we had seen spring and winter face to face; for on one side of the lake the mountains trailed their white coverings down to the water's edge, while just across the wild flowers were out in great profusion, and vegetation was springing into life.

We could see the Righi from our window, with numerous hotels on its summit and a railroad running all the way up, while in our rear was Pilatus, a much higher mountain, and a more beautiful one, I thought, especially at dawn and sunset. It is not so noted, however, on account of its inaccessibility.

As a matter of course we got some eidelweiss, though I cannot boast that we gathered it ourselves. Susie and I were very glad to be able to add this celebrated flower to our fast-growing floral collections.

We could not remain in one place always, though ever so delightful, and the time came at last to leave this queen of all the Swiss cities, beautiful Lucerne! On and on we journeyed past more "views," until, almost intoxicated with the excess of beauty, we finally stopped at Berne, where a delightful surprise awaited us in the shape of a package of mail.

Berne was such a curious old place that I felt almost as though transported again to one of the Oriental cities, especially when I began to note the disagreeable odors that greeted us during our first walk through the town. Among other interesting objects passed was a most peculiar fountain, representing a battered-up old *ogre* with a bag full of plump little babies swung on his back, while he held in his hand a chubby tot whose head he was biting off with evident relish. I had always longed to go to Berne and bring away with me some kind of a *bear*. My wish was at last gratified, and I became the happy possessor of several of these celebrated bruins, among them a cute little wooden one for my watch-chain, and another standing on his hind feet holding up a match-case.

We went out to the principal place of interest in the city, the bear-pit, and were highly entertained watching and feeding the four shaggy occupants. It was very amusing to see the great brown fellows stand up on their hind legs and wave their paws in the air, looking up most beseechingly, then lying down flat on their backs and begging for the bread which we threw them. Although they were so comical and sleepy-looking, we were told that some time before a man who was trying to recover an umbrella he had dropped into the pit fell in himself, and the bears immediately proceeded to make a meal of him, and finished the job in a very short time.

BEAR-PIT.

(336)

Parliament was in session during our visit to Berne, and every place was crowded. All up and down the streets were numerous little booths, with various articles for sale. At the fountains along the way were numbers of wash-women busy at their trade—a very necessary sort of occupation in this place, for Berne was offensively dirty.

From the terrace in the rear of the hotel we could see quite a long stretch of country, the view made especially beautiful by a sight of the Bernese Alps, with the Jungfrau conspicuous.

Berne means "a bear," consequently almost every thing in the city has some reference to that solemn and ungainly animal. They figure everywhere, and we saw bronze bears, wooden bears, candy bears, and even *gingerbread* bears, until almost tempted to make good our escape, like little "Golden Hair" in the story, and flee for our lives from the dominions of the "growlers." We did get away in safety, however, after seeing all the sights, and on the whole enjoyed exceedingly our visit to the queer old bear-town.

CHAPTER XXXIV.

INTERLACHEN—LAUSANNE—GENEVA.

THE steamer "Stadt Berne" took us the whole length of the beautiful little Lake Thun, and then, boarding the train again, we were quickly whirled on to Interlachen, where we settled ourselves at the Hotel Victoria—about the best in the place—highly delighted with our surroundings. From the windows was a fine view of the stately "Jungfrau" rearing its snow-covered head high up above the surrounding peaks.

After a walk almost as far as Lake Brienz, and to the little souvenir shops where we purchased a number of alpenstocks, Susie and I concluded to go over to the foot of the "Jungfrau" and gather some wild flowers. Taking with us our stout alpenstocks, and bidding the rest of the party wait for us on the road, we started across the level valley in the direction of the mountains. On and on we walked, toiling over the rough fields, and, strange to say, apparently getting little nearer the end of our journey than when it began. I hesitate to say how many weary miles we must have tramped, plodding determinedly on, until at last the goal was nearly reached, when, alas for our perseverance! just at the foot of the mountain we had been so long approaching, we "came to a river, and couldn't get across," even if we had been willing to "give five dollars for an old gray horse." It was a swift, jolly little mountain stream that bade us defiance as it rippled, gurgled, and tumbled over its rocky bed, seeming to chuckle with merriment over our disappointment. How we disliked to stop, with that delectable mountain almost within reach, "so near and yet so far!" But the bridge was a mile or two up the river, we were completely worn out, and our patience exhausted; so, gathering a few leaves and blossoms from the banks of the mocking stream, we sadly and wearily retraced our steps.

Hurrying back through the gathering dusk,

we found Uncle Robert starting out in search of us, and he was heartless enough to *laugh* at our discomfiture. That night we were as tired a pair of pedestrians as ever attempted to scale a mountain, while, to add to our disgust and chagrin, we found next morning, upon investigation, that the elevation we had so nearly reached was not the *Jungfrau* at all, but some similar eminence that we had mistaken for it.

On the return trip from Interlachen we went over the route on the same steamer; but the trip was much enlivened by the presence of a number of Swiss mountaineers, many of them young boys, on their way to America, expecting to be joined by one hundred and seventy others at Berne. It was a lively crowd. Only their leader could speak a little English, and nearly all of them were tipsy. They invited Uncle Robert to have some of their Swiss whisky, and, when he refused, assured him they "would treat him to beer when they got to Berne." Many of them had pieces of eidelweiss stuck in their hats, and all were dressed in the coarsest and roughest clothes.

There was an English boy on the steamer carrying with him to his home in London a beautiful St. Bernard dog, that he had bought at one of the villages. It was a cunning black-and-white puppy, and we girls soon made friends with the little master; and being especially fond of dogs, I was sorely tempted to find one to bring home myself.

Stopping at Berne only long enough to get the baggage, we had another pleasant journey to Lausanne, passing some very fine scenery on the way. Running for quite a long distance through a deep tunnel, and suddenly speeding out into the sunshine, there burst on our sight an entrancing view of Lake Leman (Geneva). We were high on the side of a cliff, and, far below, the lake shone in the sun like turquoise, with the water's edge lined with charming villages, and the mountains above a perfect net-work of fields and steep-terraced vineyards.

The Gibbon Hotel, at which we stopped in

SWISS VIEW.

Lausanne, was so called because in its garden Edward Gibbon finished his celebrated "Decline and Fall of the Roman Empire." Our windows looked out on the lake, and we were told that the season had suddenly jumped from winter to summer, with very scant chance given to spring; so the face of the whole country was smiling under the beaming rays of the sun.

We took a long drive up and down the almost perpendicular streets of the city, visited the new Palace of Justice, saw all the sights, drove down to the wharf on the lake, and took passage on the "Dauphin" for Geneva.

The weather favored our ride, and, after enjoying another series of charming Swiss scenes, we came, at the end of three hours, in sight of Mont Blanc and Geneva.

The "Sweitzer Hoff" was a delightful place to rest, and with the aid of a package of mail we soon made ourselves thoroughly happy, and once more settled down to "housekeeping."

Geneva is the finest and I suppose the cleanest city in Switzerland, and we immediately fell in love with its beauties, especially after several extremely interesting **visits to** the music-box factories, with which the place abounds. For several hours we **reveled** in melody, and it was hard to tear ourselves away. There were boxes of all shapes and sizes—little Swiss **chalets** with machinery inside **that** played tunes when the roof was raised, **chairs** that played when sat upon, albums that played when opened, door-knobs **that played when turned, birds that sung,** boxes that sounded **like organs, besides all sorts of cups,** glasses, **bowls, clocks, vases,** ink-stands, **and desks that emitted the sweetest of sounds upon change of position.** The finest of **all were** the grand orchestral boxes, which were as large as small pipe-organs, and played whole operas straight through in such a spirited manner, with every instrument so distinct that if our eyes had been shut we would scarcely have believed we were not listening to a perfectly trained orchestra of thirty or forty pieces. One of the funniest musical devices was an orchestra of bears, one of which, wearing a pair of spectacles, played **on a** hand-organ, all the time turning his head from side to side in the most comical way imaginable; another beat the drum and played on a pair of cymbals, while a third marched solemnly up and down, keeping step to the music as he walked; still another alternately raised himself up and then fell down, rolling his eyes about and snapping his jaws most ferociously. It was an amusing company of performers, and afforded us a hearty laugh as we watched their antics.

On Sunday morning Mary Green, Susie, and I went to church at the English chapel, where there was a great deal of service, but very little sermon, while Uncle Robert heard a discourse in French at the church where John Calvin used to preach. Almost everybody in Geneva spoke French, and the appearance of things in general was once more decidedly *Frenchy.*

We saw from our window several times, a little turn-out that was pretty enough to set any child wild with delight: a tiny open carriage, or brett, made just like the real "grown-up" ones, with two seats below, and one above for the driver, and drawn by two gentle-looking goats. The little folks gathered about it in crowds, and many were the wistful glances directed toward the dainty trap and pair.

Out in the middle of the river Rhone, **with** bridges running diagonally from each **bank,** was a small pleasure-garden or park, called Rousseau's **Island, on which was a** statue of that famous author and philosopher.

After **visiting Calvin's house and church, and going through a watch manufactory, where** they showed **us some works they had made** for Tiffany, **New York, and others for our Nashville jeweler, Mr. Stief, we girls were each made happy by the purchase of a lovely little gold watch with our names engraved on the cases, to take home as souvenirs of this most delightful city of time-pieces. We could not leave Geneva without visiting the shops, but as we went through an unexplored part of the city on** the way, Susie and I, strange **to say, found it rather agreeable than otherwise.**

Just below the bridge on the Rhone, workmen were engaged draining part of the river, and already it had been forced into a channel about half its original width. We watched, with a great deal of interest, a man in diving armor, who was busy about something at the bottom of the stream. When he came to the top, as he occasionally did for air, he seemed perfectly exhausted, and the rest had to help him off with his heavy suit.

There were several wash-houses, floating and stationary, on the river, where long rows of women stood behind boards, scrubbing and beating the clothes with paddles. We were told that they had to pay ten centimes (about two cents) each for the use of the boards in the houses. There was also a floating swimming-school and bath-house close by.

Next morning we rode out through the suburbs, where every thing was beautifully green and fresh, and took our last look at this charming city of the Swiss.

CHAPTER XXXV.
PARIS AGAIN.

WE were assured and re-assured by the guards at the railroad station in Geneva that there would be "no stop or change of cars until arriving at Paris;" so we settled ourselves comfortably in the coupe, with bags, bundles, and baskets to the number of eighteen pieces, for a long all-night journey to the French capital.

We had divested ourselves of hats and wraps, and were just dozing contentedly, when the monotony of things was rudely broken by the sudden throwing open of the door and the appearance of the conductor, who hurriedly shouted something in our ears. We felt quite bewildered, and sat still trying to comprehend what was expected of us, the official meanwhile becoming frantic in his jabbering and gesticulations. We at last concluded it would

be better to leave the car and find out the
trouble, so hastily threw on shoes, collars,
cuffs, hats, veils, jackets, and cloaks, while
everybody grabbed the baggage of everybody
else and made a rush for the door. Uncle Robert left *all* his things in his haste, and dashed
down the steps with a *pillow* which he had
rented for Aunt Anna's comfort during the
night. The guard insisted that it be left in
the car, whereupon followed a most animated
discussion in French and English as to whether
the pillow should go or stay, finally ending in
our party triumphantly bearing it off, together
with all the baskets, umbrellas, alpenstocks,
shawls, and hand-bags. My hat had become
somewhat caved in at the top during the exit,
and all of us looked decidedly sleepy, and much
as though suddenly "scared up." Marching
on, having no idea where, we found that they
only wanted us to step out for a few minutes
and witness the usual custom-house examination of the valises. That being over, we filed
back, *pillow* and all, and took our places in the
same coupe, feeling relieved that the trouble

was over. But alas for human hopes! We had hardly gotten things arranged again to our satisfaction, and had not finished laughing over the exciting incident, when the train stopped, the door swung open, and the guard shouted once more something that sounded like "Charnge!" In a moment all was confusion. We donned our wraps, grabbed the baggage, climbed out of the car, and following the conductor, made our way to the other side of the station, where we stood waiting for something, we knew not what. Presently another train came thundering along, into which we were hurried, and left to rest in peace for the remainder of the journey.

Arriving at the Hotel de Rohan, in Paris, we were told that "Mr. Eastman, his wife, and Mr. John Eastman (who had come over from Nashville to join them) had left there only the day before."

Our room windows looked upon the Avenue de l'Opera, with the Grand Opera House at the end of the street, and altogether a more desirable location could not have been found in the city. Just across on one side was the Louvre, and on the other the Palais Royal.

After so many months of constant travel we found ourselves in the condition of Miss Flora McFlimsy, with "nothing to wear," and it was absolutely necessary to do some shopping before going farther.

I have mentioned before that shopping was a bore to me, and I found it especially so in a great city like Paris, where there was so much of interest to be seen, and so many things of far more importance to engage the attention. I could not help feeling that every moment spent in the stores was just so much time lost, and counted every dress I was *not to get* as that much gained, being delighted when my few necessary purchases were made and I could return to the palaces and art galleries.

The largest shops, or stores, were the Bon Marche and the Magazin du Louvre. In the former, Susie and I managed to get lost one day, and it was more than an hour before our party found us, though we had the clerks running about and ringing bells at a great rate.

It was a queer experience to be lost within the walls of a store.

The first Sunday of our stay was May-day, and a *fête-time* with the French. All the fountains were in full play at Versailles, and many people were going out to see them. It was raining, so we did not attend service at any of the churches, but spent the day quietly within doors.

Next day we visited the celebrated establishment of Worth, where we saw many handsome costumes, the cheapest of which was worth seven hundred francs—about one hundred and forty dollars—quite a moderate price for that king of dress-makers.

Our various walks and drives about the city took us through the Rue Richelieu, the Rue Vivienne, across the Seine, out on the Champs Elysees, many times up and down our own street, De l'Opera, and the Rue de Rivoli. We went often to a fat, jolly dress-maker's, who had only a limited vocabulary of English, and many of our attempts at conversation were ludicrous in the extreme. She remarked, in great astonishment, when trying on one of our dresses a week or two after taking measurements, "*O, you cooms tinner!*" which was rather an original way of saying "You have fallen off," while another one was told, "*You cooms ticker*" for "You have gained flesh."

We met in the dining *salon* one day Miss Smith, the young lady who had been with us at Frau von Schack's in Berlin. She was in the city with her mother, having recently returned from a trip through Italy.

The crown jewels were on exhibition at the Louvre during most of our stay in Paris, and we went over to see them. Such a magnificent display I had no idea existed in any one collection. They were valued at ten million francs, and before we left were sold publicly to various parties—Tiffany, of New York, obtaining several handsome pieces. It seemed a pity to separate such a splendid assortment, but the people were anxious to do away with all signs of royalty, and only a few of the most valuable and historic ones were reserved by the government. These jewels were kept in a glass case that was lowered every night by machinery into a vault for safe keeping.

Uncle Robert went one day to the Hotel St. Petersburg, where we staid during our former visit to Paris, and found it full of guests, the first floor being occupied by an Indian prince and his retinue, and the second by an English nobleman and suite.

It was laughable to see us hurrying about the streets, dashing along to keep up with the crowds, and dodging from one side to the other to avoid being run over. The people seemed to vastly prefer walking or driving *over* one to going *round*, and we had to be always on the alert to prevent their doing so.

The Luxembourg Galleries, Notre Dame, and the Palace of the Louvre were again visited, besides most of the public gardens, parks, and squares.

One morning while we were at "coffee," Susie, who was sitting near the window, called us to "come and look!" There, on the Rue de Rivoli, was a tiny little donkey—hitched to a cart piled up with straw—rearing and pitching about like a wild horse. I never saw such antics: he first stood straight up on his hind feet, while his enraged old master tried to hold him down, then kept pawing and biting at the man, who slapped him soundly several times, first on one jaw and then on the other, while the straw flew in all directions, and the people on the street roared with laughter. For some time it was a regular pitched battle, and the two participants seemed to have equal chances of victory. Finally the little fellow must have gotten tired or grown ashamed of his undignified behavior, for he suddenly quieted down and allowed himself to be led off through the archway of the Louvre, looking so solemn and meek that he would never have been suspected of such frisky naughtiness. I think he must have come to the conclusion all at once that it was time for him to *strike*, and he *struck!*

Pleasure seemed the main object with these gay Parisians, and the public gardens were favorite places for seeking it. These were beautifully laid out, with grass, trees, flowers, fountains, and statuary, and were thronged with children who seemed "as happy as the days are long." One afternoon, in the garden of the Palais Royal, we stopped to watch a Punch and Judy show, and a little farther on saw a company of boys having fine fun sailing their boats on the pool around one of the fountains. It would appear, however, that the majority of the people are little better than heathens; indeed, a heathen is less guilty than one of these enlightened sinners. There is such utter disregard for the Sabbath, so many dreadful scenes enacted, and altogether so much wickedness in plain view, that one is constantly shocked and grieved by the sight, and cannot help thinking how sad it is that such a beautiful place should be the home of an almost godless people!

Packing up every thing and sending one trunk on to New York, we left Paris after a stay of three weeks, crossing the channel from Dieppe to New Haven. We lay down on our berths just before midnight—the ladies all in one cabin—and thus got a little sleep before morning. At five o'clock the steamer started, and we "all with one accord" awoke, and then began the horrors! Everybody near us was sick except the stewardess, and even the officers admitted that it was "pretty rough and choppy." The vessel rolled and pitched, while the wind blew a veritable gale, and we concluded that this was certainly the worst experience of all our various spells of "*mal de mer.*" I did not learn the name of the dreadful steamer, and have never cared to know. All I wanted was just to get off and away from it. How happy we were when at last New Haven was reached! and what sweet music it was to hear the guards, porters, and railroad officials *speaking English!* For eight long months we had been as "foreigners in a strange land," rarely hearing our mother-tongue except as we spoke to each other. Now the welcome sound made our hearts rejoice, and soon our seasick bodies were refreshed and strengthened, making us feel that this was the next best thing to reaching America.

CHAPTER XXXVI.

LONDON.

WE arrived in London at three o'clock P.M., leaving the cars at Victoria Station. The first thing that attracted our attention on the way to the hotel was the number of posters and flaming placards advertising "Buffalo Bill" and his "Wild West Show." They told us that nearly everybody in London had been to see the cowboys and Indians, from the Queen down to the cab-drivers.

On reaching the Inns of Court we saw a number of familiar faces, and were given the same rooms occupied by us when there before. The porters and chamber-maids remembered us, and even the furniture had a home look. We dined at an early hour, retired before dark, and did not breakfast next morning until after ten o'clock, thus giving ourselves a good rest after the exhausting trip across the channel.

During the morning Uncle Robert went down to Cook's office, and met there Mr. Dattari. He was stopping in London for awhile between trips, and called to see us that evening. He had been over the Egypt and Palestine tour, since leaving us, with a party of thirty-two, and gave a most graphic description of their hazardous landing at Jaffa, besides numerous adventures on the way through the Holy Land.

The weather was foggy and cloudy, so that a glimpse of the sun was rare, and we were inclined to agree with the young Englishman who pronounced it "beastly." One day it snowed quite briskly for awhile, which was rather wintery, we thought for the twentieth of May. By way of contrast, the letters from home reported the weather as being very warm "on that side."

Expecting to begin the homeward journey in a few days, and, concluding it would be better to get through with the heaviest packing first, we proceeded at once to fill the large boxes and trunks, and put them out of the way.

It was no small undertaking, and we heartily rejoiced when it was accomplished, and sight-seeing in London could be resumed.

Sunday morning we went to hear Mr. Spurgeon the second time, and were more than ever impressed by his wonderful power in the pulpit. We had heard the finest cathedral organs, the most beautiful choir music, solemn chants and grand oratorios, but nothing in all Europe to compare in soul-inspiring melody with the simple gospel hymns, sung by that immense congregation, with no organ or instrument of any kind, only the voices of the multitude blending together in a volume of praise that was impressive and comforting beyond description. We had seats quite near the preacher, and heard distinctly every word of his discourse, which occupied forty-five minutes, but did not seem half so long. The text was Mark iv. 40 : "And he said unto them, Why are ye so fearful? how is it that ye have no faith?" In the evening Uncle Robert went to hear Canon Farrar.

We had now returned to the land of regular

meat breakfasts, but during our travels had become so accustomed to a simple morning meal of coffee and chocolate, with cold bread and butter, that we really did not care for any thing else. The first morning we were served with beef-steak, ham, eggs, potatoes, and the usual coffee, tea, chocolate, and rolls, it seemed to me I had never seen such abundance. The sight of so much to eat quite took away my appetite, and I could not partake of any of the "extras." The second morning it was all I could do to force myself to eat a bit of ham and an egg. So much had habit done for me in the space of a few months.

Monday we ladies began again the interminable shopping, spending most of the time on Oxford Street. In the afternoon Mr. Dattari came by and accompanied us to the American Exhibition, the principal feature of which was Buffalo Bill's Wild West Show. There was an immense audience present, and we were told that they often took in as much as ten thousand dollars at one performance. We were highly entertained by the Indians, bucking ponies, cow-boys, and shooting. On the way out we noticed a crowd of people gathered around a little tent, and on going nearer discovered the interest to be centered in a regular black, thick-lipped negro, who was busily engaged *popping corn* and selling it to the crowd. Very few of them had ever seen pop-corn before, and were anxious to taste the American delicacy. It was rolled into balls, stuck together with sugar. Mr. Dattari, to whom it was something entirely new, suggested that it must be the sugar that made it so white. The old darky kept calling out, while the corn was popping: "Come right 'long, an' see how it's made; as white as snow, an' sweet as honey; don't go 'way widout gittin' some." And he drove a thriving trade, as did also the ice-cream-candy man.

I observed nothing in the American exhibition room particularly new or interesting, except numerous patent sewing-machines, a striking array of false teeth, and some fancy arrangements of ears of corn (something also unknown to the English). Some of the latter were made up into dainty little thermometers, tied with bows of bright ribbon, while others were fashioned into dolls, with clothes made of shucks and the hair of corn silks, besides many other devices, showing considerable taste and ingenuity.

Tuesday morning was spent at Whitely's great bazaar; and, upon returning, we stopped for awhile in Hyde Park to see the fine turn-outs and horseback riders on Rotten Row. I cannot say much for the grace of English girls on horseback; their principal object seemed to be to *hold on*, while their sturdy cobs, with tails cropped short, went jolting along in a back-breaking trot or gallop.

On one of the streets near the hotel was Charles Dickens's "Old Curiosity Shop," an ancient, queer-looking building, now used as a waste-paper warehouse, and looking so much as the great novelist described it that I would scarcely have been surprised to see "Little Nell" lead her grandfather out of the door.

The climb to the top of St. Paul's Cathedral—only three hundred and seventy-five

ST. PAUL'S CATHEDRAL.

(364)

steps—was a little disappointing after Cologne, St. Peter's, and Milan, and the view was not particularly good on account of the irrepressible London mist, or fog; but we enjoyed very much the old library of nine thousand volumes, and the Whispering Gallery—the best thing of the kind we had heard. Two additions had been made since our visit in the fall—one, a handsome marble and bronze tomb and statue of General Charles George Gordon, placed in one of the recesses of the church by his brother; the other, a white marble statue of Queen Anne, erected in front of the cathedral.

Friday morning was spent in visiting the Royal Academy, and, though it was raining, we enjoyed the trip wonderfully. The gallery was crowded with people, and many of the pictures were very fine. The two that I particularly admired were "Excelsior" and "For the Safety of the Public"—both dog-pieces.

We went again to Madame Tussaud's, and found several new groups of figures, added since our former visit—among them the Queen

Regent of Spain and the infant king; and a royal jubilee group, representing **Queen Victoria** as she looked fifty years ago, dressed in her coronation robes, surrounded by her court, taking the vows in Westminster Abbey.

We were much pleased to meet, while walking about looking at the figures, our young friend **Mr. Carter**, whom we had seen in Venice; he had been in England for some time, but expected to return to America in August.

Our farewell look at London was taken under a clear sky, and we were glad to see that "Merry England" was likely to have a sunny summer after all the mist and fog of the wintery spring.

CHAPTER XXXVII.

WINDSOR—ETON—STOKE-POGIS—OXFORD.

A SHORT ride brought us to Windsor, the chief attraction of which was the castle, or "Carstle," as the English call it. We were just in time to see the interior of the building, as it was to be closed on the following day, owing to preparations being made for the jubilee celebration.

Fortunately the weather was fine, and we saw it to the best advantage, finding it even grander and more castle-like than we had imagined. The Memorial, or Albert Chapel, was beautiful, as was also the tomb of Princess Charlotte, carved out of pure white marble, with a lovely effect in color produced by a flood of yellow light that poured over it from the stained glass window. We climbed to the top of the round tower, and had a fine view of the castle grounds, parks, and surrounding

WINDSOR CASTLE.

country; visited the royal stables, and then the state apartments, chief of which were St. George's Hall, the grand reception-room, and the Waterloo Chamber.

Next day we entered an open carriage, and drove the whole length of what is called the Long Walk, a distance of three miles, from the castle to the statue of George III., passing first through the Queen's private park, and then the great Windsor Park. In the latter were five thousand deer, many of them so tame they scarcely noticed our carriage, even when it passed close to them. On the way we met a vehicle in which were seated two ladies, one of whom was Princess Eleanor, daughter of Queen Victoria and wife of Prince Christian, of Schleswig-Holstein—a rather pretty, stylish-looking lady, with nothing remarkable about her, however, except her royal birth and marriage.

Queen Anne's Drive was a delightful one, extending for several miles through a thickly shaded grove of English oaks, the road-way covered with velvety turf.

Riding past Eton College we saw numbers of students on the streets, going, we supposed, to their various classes. The little fellows in the lower forms were dressed in *bob-tailed* jackets, tall stove-pipe hats, broad white collars, and long trousers, only the boys in the higher classes being allowed skirts to their coats. Uncle Robert was much amused when I happened to remark that these small boys reminded me forcibly of the little dog in the song, only they had their "*coats* cut short and their *hats* cut long." The founder's boys wore gowns and "mortar-boards"—a somewhat more dignified costume. They all board in the houses of the tutors, who are not allowed to take more than forty at one time. The different classes have separate play-grounds, and one would think ought to be happy and contented with such beautiful surroundings.

Next we drove out to Stoke-Pogis, a little country church, the grave-yard of which furnished Gray the subject for his "Elegy;" and just such a quiet, peaceful spot as one would imagine it—quaint and picturesque, the walls overgrown with ivy, and the whole kept in perfect order. The turf-covered graves were gayly sprinkled with wild flowers, of which we gathered a quantity, while the old sexton gave us several sprays from the yew-tree beneath which Gray sat when writing his famous poem. Inside the church was the tomb of Thomas Penn and others of his kindred; and the stone baptismal font was beautifully decorated with wreaths and clusters of sweet-smelling blossoms. The poet's grave was outside not far from the ivy-covered walls, and a more quiet place for the final sleep could not be desired. Continuing our drive, we passed Stoke Park, once the home-place of William Penn, while near Stoke-Pogis the celebrated English jurist Sir Edmund Coke had his residence, dying there in 1634. The whole route led us through some of the most charming portions of England, and the country looked its prettiest as we wound through shady lanes where the wild flowers grew in profusion, each side of the way being lined with beautiful hawthorne hedges, diffusing a delightful fragrance from the great clusters of snow-white blooms.

Soon after arriving in Oxford we made our way to the "Roe Buck" Hotel, and did full justice to its comfortable accommodations and savory fare.

Next morning, with the assistance of a guide, we took in the sights of the place, going first to Lincoln College, where John Wesley was once a Fellow, visiting the famous Bodleian Library, comprising, I suppose, the most valuable collection in the world; also the Radcliffe Library, where from the top of the building we had a fine view of the city. After going into one other library—that in Merton College, the oldest collection of books in existence—we went to Christ Church College, which was the largest of all, and had at that time two hundred and fifty students. They allowed us to look into the kitchen and pantries, and we were much interested in observing their neat and orderly appointments. This college was founded by Cardinal Wolsey, and its chapel, with a richly-carved ceiling, was especially attractive. We went to Magdalen College and saw Addison's Walk, which was indeed a charming retreat, heavily shaded, ornamented with flowering plants, and keeping close to the bank of a cunning little river that gurgled merrily along on its way to the busy Thames. It was at Oriel College that "Tom Brown" is said to have been a pupil while "at Oxford." In all, there were twenty-one colleges and more than three thousand students, many of whom we saw sauntering about dressed in black gowns and "mortar-boards."

In the afternoon Mary Green, Susie, and I went out to Summertown, a suburb of Oxford, where I delivered to Mrs. Roush a package that had been intrusted to me by her brother, a gentleman in Columbia. We enjoyed the walk greatly, and on the way back passed the Martyrs' Memorial, erected in memory of Ridley, Cranmer, and Latimer.

I admired exceedingly the cozy little English homes, and was especially impressed with the evident fondness for flowers displayed by even the poorest people. No thatched cottage seemed too wretched and mean for a small bed or stand of bright plants, and I could not but wish that our own people were more like the English in this respect.

I am sure we would all have enjoyed a longer stay in this charming city of colleges, but there were other places and things to be seen, so we again took up the line of march.

CHAPTER XXXVIII.

LEAMINGTON—KENILWORTH—STRATFORD.

THE day after arriving at Leamington, having arranged for rooms at the "Temperance Hotel," we drove out in an open carriage to Warwick Castle, the first view of which was from a bridge over the little river Avon—about the smallest stream to be called a river we had seen, and must have been dignified with the name during a freshet.

A short walk up the shady drive from the entrance gate brought us to the castle, the exterior of which was especially fine. In the state apartments were the customary paintings, statuary, and relics. The present Earl of Warwick—as is usually the case—was away from England at that time. The views from every window were superb, and I found myself wondering how the earl, with so lovely a home, could make up his mind to such habit-

WARWICK CASTLE.

ual absence. The building, viewed from the outside, was an ideal castle, situated as it is upon the banks of the swift-flowing Avon, with its rugged walls softened and harmonized by the ivy that creeps over them, making a picture of surpassing charm.

A sunny sky smiled down upon us next morning, and we took advantage of the pleasant weather by driving out to the ruins of Kenilworth Castle. All along the way were neat little sidewalks bordering the country roads, these being shaded by trees, their leafy branches meeting across the way, while again the fragrant hawthorne added its sweetness and beauty to the scene. Kenilworth was a picturesque pile of ivy-covered ruins, and we girls climbed all over and around it, exploring hidden nooks and corners. It was such a delightful day that a great many people from surrounding towns and villages were out, among them a crowd of boys belonging to a Sunday-school excursion, who made the old walls rings with their fun and merriment. We considered Kenilworth perfect just as it

SHAKESPEARE'S BIRTHPLACE.

(378)

was, and ventured the hope that nobody would try to "restore" it, for certainly no addition could be made to its matchless beauty.

Returning to Leamington for rest, we went again by carriage to Stratford, passing on the way the old Lucy estate, where, in the days of Sir Thomas Lucy, William Shakespeare's deer-stealing escapade is said to have occurred.

In Stratford we secured rooms at the "Red Horse" Hotel, a queer, old-fashioned inn, where Washington Irving staid during his visit to the place. They showed us his parlor, also his chair and poker, the latter instrument carefully "done up" in a silk case.

Just across from our hotel was the "Old Red Lion," and next door the "Golden Lion." We walked to Shakespeare's house, which looked much as the pictures represent it, with its quaint old double door—the upper half a kind of shutter, and within numerous pieces of clumsy and ancient furniture. The "best-room," pantry, kitchen, and the upstairs-room —in which "Immortal Will" was born—were all shown us, the rest of the house being used as a museum, where were displayed various relics of the great writer—his signet ring, different editions of his works, his jug, a cup made from his mulberry-tree, and a portrait of him taken from life. This last is considered so valuable a treasure that it is locked up every night in a fire-proof safe. On one of the small window-panes of the room where Shakespeare was born is the name of "Walter Scott," said to have been cut by the novelist himself with the stone in his diamond ring. The windows bore a good many other names, though not all so illustrious.

The old stone church was then visited, and as service was being conducted, we remained until it was over. It was the day before Trinity, and they were decorating the altar and chancel with flowers for the occasion, making the place especially attractive. Besides William Shakespeare's tomb, which is here, we also saw those of Anne Hathaway, his wife, and Judith (Mrs. Hall), his daughter. One of the beautiful stained glass windows overlooking the great poet's last resting-place was contributed by American admirers, and is indeed a lovely and appropriate tribute to his memory. Outside the old grave-yard, beautifully kept and adorned with flowers, sloped down to the Avon, and the whole made a quiet, peaceful spot for the last long sleep. Not far from the church, and near the river, was a pretty and picturesque building, which we were told was the "Shakespeare Memorial Theater."

On our return we stopped at the Shakespeare Hotel, all the rooms in the house being named for his different plays—the dining-room called "As You Like It," the drawing-room "Much Ado about Nothing," and the office "All's Well that Ends Well." A short distance out from Stratford still stands the small thatched cottage where once lived Anne Hathaway.

Returning on Sunday to Leamington, we worshiped at a little Primitive Methodist chapel just across the street from the hotel. The building was not elegant or costly—only a plain, country-like church—but the service was a real Methodist one, with a good, honest, practical sermon, and hearty congregational singing. It is hardly necessary to state the fact that we ritual-wearied travelers heartily enjoyed the simplicity and earnestness of a service that we could understand and be profited by.

CHAPTER XXXIX.

CHESTER—LIVERPOOL.

A DELIGHTFUL trip through part of Wales brought our party finally to Chester. Among other interesting places passed on the way was Birmingham—that dingy, busy, manufacturing city, which its inhabitants call the "work-shop of the world." It seemed a perfect forest of tall chimney-stacks, or *stalks*, as the people style them, while a pall of smoke hung over the place, giving it a decidedly gloomy aspect.

Eaton Hall is the country seat of the Duke of Westminster, whose estate is about five miles square, and we drove out from Chester one morning to visit it. Every thing was arranged and appointed on a scale of extraordinary magnificence. The Duke is immensely rich, having an income of £2 5*s a minute*, but is very generous withal, and several charities were pointed out which his liberality had established.

A long drive through the shady park brought us to the Hall, which, in contrast to most of the places we had heretofore seen, was fitted up in *modern* style. A most attractive apartment was the grand library, containing eleven thousand volumes, besides a magnificent organ and a great deal of handsome furniture. The paneling of the walls and book-cases in this room was of oak, inlaid richly with mother-of-pearl, while a tall, carved, mantel cabinet bearing the family arms served to complete an effect that was unusually tasteful and elegant. Many of the volumes were bound in vellum and gold, and to a lover of books formed the principal attraction of this royal treasure-house. Passing through halls beautifully decorated with costly marbles, rare bric-a-brac, and innumerable gems of art, we were conducted into the chapel, and shown the tombs of several members of the family. The whole establishment, with its surroundings, was perfect in design and beauty, lacking nothing that money or taste could provide for its adornment, and I found myself wondering once more that people who own such lovely homes should leave them and remain away so much of the time, and why this should be the case the world over.

We drove through a good many streets in Chester, and were struck with the queer arrangement of the shops. The "rows," as they were called, extended along even with the second stories of the business houses, and were really arcades, on which were situated most of the principal stores of the city. It was a novel experience to go "down-town" and do all the shopping upstairs.

A church and a school built by the Duke of Westminster were pointed out, and they told us that all the fees taken at the Hall were devoted to charitable purposes.

The time had now come for our last railroad journey before the departure for home, and we took the train for Liverpool, from which place we were to embark. This is a noisy, busy town, resembling our American cities in its hurry and bustle. Crossing the ferry over the river Mersey, our attention was directed to the largest vessel ever constructed—the "Great Eastern," lying at anchor in the harbor. It certainly was a huge affair, and beside it the rest of the ships and smaller craft seemed little more than toy-boats.

Uncle Robert went on board the "Etruria," on which we had engaged passage home, examined state-rooms etc., and reported every thing in good order. This steamer was the *twin* of the "Umbria," and at that time about the fastest on the water—in fact, had made the quickest one-hour's record ever known.

We went down to the principal square of the city, where is situated St. George's Hall, and after walking along the front, examining the equestrian statues of Queen Victoria and Prince Albert, also a statue of Disraeli, entered the handsome building, and found the hall, which is used for concerts and balls, quite a spacious and elegant room. There were two fine stained glass windows, representing St. George slaying the dragon, and besides, a large pipe-organ and numerous statues of celebrated persons. The outside was so blackened and discolored (I suppose by smoke and the effect of sea-air) that it was almost impossible to tell of what material the edifice was constructed. In this square was also a magnificent column erected in honor of Wellington and Waterloo.

We were surprised and somewhat inconvenienced by the scarcity of dry goods stores, as we had some necessary purchases to make in preparing for the voyage; there were gentlemen's furnishing establishments in abundance, but I should hesitate to say how many blocks had to be traversed before we could find a place where they kept even ordinary *pins*.

There were very few ladies on the streets, the majority of the population seeming to consist of business men, rough-looking sailors, and the most wretched, miserable paupers. We had not seen so many beggars and dreadfully deformed people since leaving Italy.

The long English twilights were a constant source of wonder to us; it was something unusual to close up shutters and pull down shades, *to keep out the light*, when the time came for retiring, which with tired travelers was generally at nine o'clock.

Finally the last night on foreign shores rolled around, and we settled ourselves to sleep, sincerely hoping that next day would bring us favorable winds and waves for the beginning of our voyage across the Atlantic. We awoke to find the weather bright and pleasant, with the summer's sun aglow, and every thing in harmony with our happy thoughts of home.

All had been made ready, bundles securely tied, trunks strapped, valises coaxed into staying fastened, and we gayly made our way down to the docks, after *feeing* the numerous waiters, porters, and chamber-maids, who invariably gathered to see us off. In fact, this latter part of the preparation for departure made us feel quite in sympathy with the exasperated American tourist, who, while standing on the wharf at Liverpool, remarked in a loud tone of great disgust, just before his steamer left: "If there is a *blarsted* Englishman on this con-

founded island to whom I have not given a shilling let him come now and get it, for *this is his larst charnce.*"

After waiting for several hours, a small tug conveyed our party with a number of other passengers out to the "Etruria," where we soon found our state-rooms, and arranged things in order for the voyage.

There was hardly as much excitement when the vessel left as we had noticed on our departure from New York, but there was enough to keep up interest until half-past two o'clock, when the anchor was weighed, and we found ourselves once more at the tender mercy

> Of the rolling deep,
> Where the winds their revels keep.

CHAPTER XL.

THE VOYAGE HOME.

WE had found from experience that a "life on the ocean wave" has its disagreeable as well as its pleasant side, consequently it was not with unalloyed delight that we settled ourselves in the steamer chairs and watched the shores of England gradually fade from view.

The afternoon and evening were spent on deck, and really enjoyed, as the weather was fine and the atmosphere pure and bracing. When at last the time for retiring came, we listened to the noisy thud of the screw as though it had been the most harmonious music, because we knew that each revolution was carrying us nearer home and friends.

Next morning, on awaking, we found the vessel anchored just outside the harbor of Queenstown, with Erin's green shores spread before us. Taking on a number of passengers and the mail, we steamed out into the ocean again, greeting with many cheers and hurrahs the ship "Arizona," which we had seen start from Liverpool in company with the "Etruria."

At noon that day the rocking motion began, and, concluding that "discretion was the better part of valor," we girls beat a hasty retreat to our state-rooms, and before very long to our berths. On the following morning the waves were in entirely too playful a mood for comfort or pleasure on deck, so the day was spent below; and we amused ourselves as best we could with a number of books that had been provided, and our never-failing songs and games, assisted by a huge bag of lemons and a corresponding one of loaf-sugar, though for such active, vigorous young people lying all day in a berth soon grew to be monotonous. The fog-horn had been sounding for several hours, and we were told that the decks were deserted by the passengers on account of a disagreeable drizzle.

Things looked somewhat better next morning, and sufficient courage was summoned to crawl above, where a greater part of the day was spent, though we did not dare venture again to the dining-saloon.

In the afternoon the wind began to rise, and before the sun went down we had to give up the second time, and dark found us "fallen and prostrate" within the narrow confines of our berths. Soon after we had retired old Neptune got on quite a "lark," and the winds and waves were so rough that the steamer performed a most uncomfortable *seesawing* diversion — any thing but fun to us. First, climbing to the crest of a mountain wave, there would be an instant's pause; and then, losing all hold, the ship would go plunging down, down, down, with a crunching sort of sound which almost convinced me several times that we had struck the rocks at the bottom. Though the timbers creaked, and every bolt and screw seemed strained, the brave "Etruria" always righted herself and came to the top at last, boldly riding the boisterous waves. I had always, hitherto, desired to witness a storm at sea, and now my wish was gratified in rather too literal a manner. I could not sleep, but held on to the sides of the berth to keep from rolling out, listening to the restless billows rushing and beating about the deck above my head, and it was daylight before I finally dropped into a doze from mere exhaustion. Fortunately, none of us were much seasick during the storm, and thus one of the usual horrors was avoided. Next day, however, the water was still very rough, and we lay in our berths suffering tortures, hoping sincerely that this might be our last experience of a "war of elements and rush of waves." Uncle Robert—the only one of us who had escaped the horrid *mal de mer*—on his return from an exploring trip to the deck, informed us that every thing was closed up, hatchways all down, port-holes shut, and the waves, which really looked "mountain high," washing over the promenade deck. The ship continued to roll so much that it was difficult to keep from being thrown from the berths, while the water, dashing up over the port, filled our room with a green, uncanny sort of light. The monotony of things was frequently relieved by the crash of broken china and glassware from the dining-saloon, but we rather enjoyed the sound of that, as the most tempting edibles would just then have been an offense to us. What a relief it was when on Thursday the sun shone out warm and bright, and we were able to make our way again to the fresh air on the upper deck! The waters were almost quiet, and only gave an occasional playful tumble, as though amused at the remembrance of the fright and discomfort their rough frolicsomeness had caused us.

We were considerably startled that afternoon when the motion of the screw, getting gradually slower and slower, finally stopped altogether, and left us almost motionless on the silent water. Nothing can be imagined more intense than the quiet of a ship at rest in mid-ocean; and while we were ruefully contemplating the probability of drifting for perhaps hours or days waiting for repairs to be made, the welcome sound was heard, and we went steaming on again, much relieved that the damage had been so easily remedied.

On Friday there was another fog, and at intervals during the afternoon the discordant sound of the horn was heard. Just about sunset it cleared off; all the clouds and mist disappeared toward the east—" gone back to London, where they belong," as Susie remarked. In the west, however—toward *home* —every thing was bright and beautiful, as we glided on in the direction of the setting sun, cheered and encouraged by the glory of its radiance and the certainty of approaching land.

The pilot from the shore came aboard at ten o'clock on Saturday, and then the all-absorbing question was, " Would the sanitary officers reach us and finish their examination in time to land that night?" Passing into the harbor of New York as dark came on, we had a good view of the Statue of Liberty holding aloft her gleaming torch, and then the anchor was cast, and we gave up the hope of getting ashore before morning. In a little while, however, a filled our room with a green, uncanny sort of light. The monotony of things was frequently relieved by the crash of broken china and glassware from the dining-saloon, but we rather enjoyed the sound of that, as the most tempting edibles would just then have been an offense to us. What a relief it was when on Thursday the sun shone out warm and bright, and we were able to make our way again to the fresh air on the upper deck! The waters were almost quiet, and only gave an occasional playful tumble, as though amused at the remembrance of the fright and discomfort their rough frolicsomeness had caused us.

We were considerably startled that afternoon when the motion of the screw, getting gradually slower and slower, finally stopped altogether, and left us almost motionless on the silent water. Nothing can be imagined more intense than the quiet of a ship at rest in mid-ocean; and while we were ruefully contemplating the probability of drifting for perhaps hours or days waiting for repairs to be made, the welcome sound was heard, and we went steaming on again, much relieved that the damage had been so easily remedied.

On Friday there was another fog, and at intervals during the afternoon the discordant sound of the horn was heard. Just about sunset it cleared off; all the clouds and mist disappeared toward the east—"gone back to London, where they belong," as Susie remarked. In the west, however—toward *home* —every thing was bright and beautiful, as we glided on in the direction of the setting sun, cheered and encouraged by the glory of its radiance and the certainty of approaching land.

The pilot from the shore came aboard at ten o'clock on Saturday, and then the all-absorbing question was, "Would the sanitary officers reach us and finish their examination in time to land that night?" Passing into the harbor of New York as dark came on, we had a good view of the Statue of Liberty holding aloft her gleaming torch, and then the anchor was cast, and we gave up the hope of getting ashore before morning. In a little while, however, a small yacht came alongside, and, greeted with shouts and cheers, the doctor and the custom-house officers were soon on board going through with their forms; after which the anchor was weighed, and we moved slowly and majestically up to the dock. Our party was standing on the deck watching eagerly for familiar faces, and when, among the surging crowd that was waiting on the pier, we recognized my father and mother and Alex. Hunter (brother of Mary Green and Susie), who had come to New York to meet us, a joyful shout went up, and we could scarcely restrain our impatience until the gangway was in place. They had also discovered us, and when at last our turn came and we filed down and made our way to them, there was indeed a happy meeting as we embraced each other with delight.

How we finally managed to get to the Grand Central Hotel, amidst all the pleasant confusion, I am not exactly sure; but it was accomplished, and we found there several other Nashville people whom it was pleasant to see. We passed a delightful evening, made all the more enjoyable by some lovely flowers which Mr. W. Kniseley, of New York, had provided for us, and a big box of American candy that was awaiting us, and which we girls devoured with an appetite whetted by long abstinence.

The hot weather was quite in contrast to the chilly sea-breezes to which we had grown accustomed, but all were so busy telling things and asking questions that we had no thought of the temperature.

In the afternoon a friend in the city accompanied us on a walk, and we heard a service in honor of Queen Victoria's Jubilee, at St. Thomas's Church, on Fifth Avenue.

Next morning our party, now increased in numbers to eight, boarded one of the Hudson River steamers and spent the day on that beautiful river, enjoying together its exquisite scenery, which reminded us of the Scotch lakes.

I shall not go into particulars of how we made stops on the way home at Albany, Niagara, Buffalo, and other places, but will hurry on to Louisville, where, standing on the platform, whom should we see but my brother,

Frank Searcy, and a cousin of ours, Mr. Frank Prentice. They had also come up to meet us, but after waiting a day or two at Cincinnati had given us out for the time, and were this far on their way home. After many happy greetings our gradually growing party continued the journey, being further re-enforced at Gallatin, Tenn., by the addition of our uncle, Captain Frank W. Green, so that when we finally reached the Union Depot at Nashville there were thirteen of us in all—two other cousins, Frank G. Fite and Thos. D. Fite, Jr., having joined us at Edgefield Station. How delighted we were as familiar landmarks began to come into view, and when at last we spied the White's Creek Turnpike and the dear old Cumberland River, our joy fairly bubbled over in enthusiastic cheers! Then the meeting at the depot! I am afraid some of the spectators must have thought it the landing of subjects for a lunatic asylum. All the Greens, Fites, Hunters, and Youngs were there, besides a host of friends, and such a tremendous hubbub was enough to startle even the "iron horse" that had brought us home. Everybody kissed everybody else promiscuously, and, if all accounts are true, two or three strange ladies received a share of the warm greeting, to their very great surprise and confusion.

Somehow we managed to find the residence of Uncle Thomas D. Fite, and there met another detachment, and the delightful confusion was increased yet more. What a bountiful supper was served, and how we hungry travelers enjoyed the delicious home fare! Next day the whole family of fathers, mothers, aunts, uncles, and cousins went out in a body to "Greenland," on White's Creek, the former home of our grandfather, Dr. A. L. P. Green, now the residence of Captain Frank W. Green. There, beneath the roof so dear to us from many hallowed associations, we gathered round the generous board to the number of thirty-two, and were bountifully feasted amid the sweet sounds of happy voices and merry laughter.

Now that the long journey was ended, our hearts went out in gratitude to our loving heavenly Father who had cared for us so tenderly, "granted us journeying mercies," and finally brought us to this happy reunion, where there was not one empty place, not one dear face missing. O that it may be typical of the last joyous meeting in our home in the great hereafter!

www.ingramcontent.com/pod-product-compliance
Lightning Source LLC
Chambersburg PA
CBHW022124290426
44112CB00008B/795